DECADES
A Century of Fashion
CAMERON SILVER

DECADES
Cameron Silver

with Rebecca DiLiberto

BLOOMSBURY
LONDON • NEW DELHI • NEW YORK • SYDNEY

Contents

Previous Two dresses designed by
Charles James in 1946—the first in
metallic shades of gray, the second
in brightest fuchsia. With their
sculptural concentric flares of stiff
taffeta, both exhibit the designer's
preternatural knack for draping
and architecture.

Right Model Penny Slinger wears
a white chiffon dress and cape
ensemble from British designer
Thea Porter's summer 1972
collection. Porter's eclectic,
high-boho style combined intricate
Middle Eastern beadwork with
unapologetic European sexuality.

Introduction

I never thought that I'd end up working in fashion. With a bachelor's degree in theater, I started my career as a modern-day interpreter of verboten Weimar cabaret songs.

The mission was to make the American public fall wildly in love with the music of 1920s and '30s Berlin. "Want to buy some illusions?" I crooned, convinced that the world was ready to embrace Friedrich Hollaender's legendary songs of political satire and social commentary. I cut an album for Hollywood Records and began touring the country, from San Francisco to Orlando to Seattle and beyond. Between gigs, I wandered from one secondhand store to another in silence, to preserve my voice. I got to know each city quietly, while looking at its sartorial castoffs.

I sought out men's pieces, ensembles to wear while performing, or to share with my natty friends. I snapped up navy YSL suits from the seventies, bright Pucci ties from the sixties, and Louis Vuitton steamer trunks from any decade at all. But wherever I went, I found more interesting women's clothes than men's, and even though I had no idea what I was going to do with these dresses—I certainly wasn't interested in wearing them—I found myself compelled to buy every single truly wonderful thing I came upon. As I sang Hollaender's "Eine Kleine Sehnsucht," which means "Just a Little Yearning" in German, I realized that I yearned to find a future for these dresses.

All the world's a stage, and I had an inkling that my own signature stage might be the floor of a vintage couture boutique, rather than a dimly lit boîte. Maybe a better way to transport my public back in time—rather than through the art of cabaret—would be to introduce them to the vintage treasures I'd found all over the world.

Thus I decided to embark on a career as a purveyor of only the finest pre-worn clothing, with one caveat—my philosophy would be to procure and sell vintage that, perhaps paradoxically, looked modern. No retro, costume aesthetic for me. While my perspective was by no means revolutionary, I did aim to cast a new spell over the used-clothing business.

In 1997, I officially retired from my cabaret concert career and opened my store on Melrose Avenue, which I called Decades. I had no experience managing a business, and no real education in fashion, other than as a consumer, but I knew that I wanted to introduce a new world of customers to vintage. Before purchasing any single piece, I would always ask myself, "Is this modern?"

In addition to offering a rarefied assortment of merchandise, I wanted to make shopping for vintage goods into the same kind of experience as buying high-end designer clothing at Barneys. I wanted to create a space that felt both authoritative and luxurious. Unlike at Barneys though, every single piece that I presented there would be one-of-a-kind. I'd be selling access to real individuality. (And, years before the global green zeitgeist, I had unwittingly found a niche for one of the first environmentally conscious luxury businesses.)

Gathering vintage inventory with which to open the store, I didn't know what to look for. While I had a very limited understanding of twentieth-century fashion, one thing I did know was what I liked—and what I didn't. It was this lack of knowledge and surplus of taste that helped my business succeed at the beginning. Instead of looking for labels or long-lost sewing techniques as vintage collectors do, I sought out the dresses that I wanted to see my most stylish girlfriends wearing. Recognizing which old pieces looked modern and which looked dated was not a skill I could have been taught—it was simply a matter of gut instinct.

People say, "Of course you have a taste for couture, you were born with a silver spoon in your mouth!" But even though I grew up in Beverly Hills, I was not raised in the lap of luxury. I was born with the ability to tell a silver spoon from a tin one with alarming accuracy, and that's what really matters.

My grandmother grew up with wealth that was lost during the Great Depression, and consequently, she was very frugal. Although my parents didn't have much money during their own childhoods, my mother and father were able to provide a wonderful life for me. I was exposed to many nice things, >

All the world's a stage, and I had an inkling that my own signature stage might be the floor of a vintage couture boutique, rather than a dimly lit boîte.

< but even more important was the fact that my adventurous parents traveled a lot—and they brought me along with them.

Because I was an only child, I was never really treated like a child at all. Although my parents didn't exactly travel in high-fashion circles, they did throw grown-up parties, and even as a kid, I was always on the guest list. I monitored what each guest wore with great interest. When I was in high school, I started to develop my eye for "good" clothes. This was the mid-1980s, when my mother started buying items from designers whose names I recognized, such as Claude Montana, Thierry Mugler, and Sonia Rykiel. This period of my mother's life was her most glamorous, and I loved every moment of it. I still remember just what she looked like in a black-and-white Valentino suit one evening when we were staying together at the Waldorf Astoria in New York. I was excited to be seen with such a chic lady. It was then that I realized I could derive great joy from seeing someone I loved look really terrific. I witnessed the incredible power possessed by a woman in her most fashionable state.

Given that I really got into fashion in the 1980s, it's funny that I long resisted selling anything from the eighties at Decades. (I simply couldn't hold out anymore—Young Hollywood sure loves its shoulder pads and micro-minis.) For years, I wondered why I had such an irrational aversion to eighties vintage fashions—until finally I realized that they weren't "vintage" to me. The eighties were the first decade that I had already experienced the first time to come back into fashion. For me, shopping the 1980s was like being forced to watch a personalized fashion version of *This Is Your Life*. Clothes from the 1980s made me feel old.

Back in the eighties, not only had I seen my mother's figure transformed by the genius architecture of a Mugler suit, but I had also worked at Theodore, a wildly expensive Beverly Hills boutique with an A-list clientele. I took a year off from college to toil full-time at the famous Beverly Center location, earning an obscene amount of money simply by charming the pants off famous people, and then selling them new ones.

At that point in my life, fashion was my paycheck, but performing was my passion. I had been recruited to study in the UCLA theater department back when I was a sophomore in high school. A faculty member saw me in a special student performance at the Ahmanson Theater, and almost immediately afterward I received a letter that said, "If you would like to come to UCLA, we would love to have you." Who could say no to such an offer? I was glad they'd recognized my star quality, and hoped—okay, expected—that they'd be the first of many in positions of power to do so.

But when I actually got to UCLA, I realized I wasn't satisfied being a theater major. I was the only one who didn't cry in acting class.

Above all, I just wanted to entertain. I am truly a performer at heart, but my act makes more sense in my boutique than it would on some off-Broadway stage. That's because my favorite—my only—role is playing myself. The one time I miss being on a "real" stage is when I watch someone really good perform: Part of my life has been missing for the thirteen years since I stopped doing my concerts, and even though I love putting on a show for my clients every day, a small part of me will always be unfulfilled.

It must be because of my performance history that I am able to develop real connections with gifted actresses. I just understand them—the simultaneous sense of elation and vulnerability they feel when they're in the public eye. My past is not something I talk about with my famous clients—most of them don't know I have a bachelor's in theater, or that I toured around the country for several years, doing some very unglamorous performances—but I like to think I understand the artist's way a little bit.

I'm very sensitive to an actress's insecurities. I understand that actresses are not models, and that sometimes they're held up to unfair standards when it comes to their physical appearance. Cultivating a flawless, fashionable persona is practically a requirement of being a famous person nowadays, but this wasn't expected of actors and actresses until as recently as fifteen years ago. The actress's job description changed when Anna

I saw this confection from across the room and found it perfect, brilliant, iconic.

Wintour began putting starlets instead of supermodels on the cover of *Vogue* magazine. In working with actresses to dress them for public appearances, I aim to help them not fear the public's expectations. I participate in the creation of effortless-seeming glamour, acknowledging that the illusion of perfection doesn't come naturally to everybody.

But I'm getting ahead of myself. I have yet to explain how I came to dress so many actresses in the first place.

On May 19, 1997, my twenty-seventh birthday, I took possession of half the ground floor of the Art Deco building on Melrose Avenue, where Decades still resides. As my real-estate agent reluctantly handed over the keys, she begged, "Please do not take this lease! This building has seen fourteen failed businesses in a row." Thank goodness I didn't listen to that real-estate agent: I now co-own the building.

My lifelong friend Patrick helped me to drag ten jam-packed rolling racks' worth of clothes into the store. (They had been stored at my mother's place—now that thousands of squatting dresses had flown the coop, she was relieved to be able to see out her windows again.) It felt as though we were playing house in that pristine space. We had no clue, so we just did what we thought we were supposed to be doing.

I opened Decades at a moment when American fashion was all about street style: basically, anti-fashion. This strategy was,

to say the least, illogical. Nowadays, people will dress to the nines to attend the opening of an envelope, but back in 1997, the one glamorous night of the year was the Oscars. These were the days when you used to see pictures of celebrities wearing Scrunchies and jean shorts on the red carpet. The days when nobody was interested in getting dressed up. But I had a feeling things were about to change.

My first major merchandising score happened in Seattle. While most everybody was walking the streets in flannel shirts, I was gently transitioning out of my cabaret phase, wearing tailored daytime suits. It was at a funny midcentury emporium called That's Atomic! that I spotted my very first vintage Dior. I saw this confection from across the room and found it perfect, brilliant, iconic. Freaking out over my find, I must have seemed absolutely insane, because the dress was not in style.

I decided to invest heavily in the New Look, a celebration of postwar glamour. Even though my fifties fascination was a tad premature, it wasn't long before Gwyneth Paltrow decided to channel Grace Kelly in pink Ralph Lauren at the Oscars, making international headlines with a polished look that seemed somehow subversive in its feminine perfection. Seeing those images, I felt a profound sense of relief. All that fancy stuff I'd been hoarding for the store would sell after all.

At the beginning, the store's design was very simple. Set against blue paneled walls were simple rolling racks—we had no permanent fixtures—on which hung scores of one-of-a-kind vintage dresses. For displaying accessories, there were some midcentury medical cabinets that I bought at a flea market. The focal point of the room was a huge framed mirror, and the spiritual center of the place was a massive, gracious dressing room.

The store got its big break when Nicole Kidman chose a couture gown by Loris Azzaro to wear to the premiere of Baz Luhrmann's *Moulin Rouge!* Overnight, pictures of Nicole looking subtle yet stunning in a white-fringed creation with delicate spaghetti straps appeared all over the world—including on the cover of *Women's Wear Daily*.

Not long after Nicole became our first well-known customer, Grace Coddington, *Vogue*'s longtime creative director, devoted eight whole pages of the magazine purely to vintage. This was a revolutionary act for the number-one fashion magazine in the world, whose primary financial goal was to satisfy advertisers by creating demand for their products. When you fill a story with dresses from days gone by, there's nothing to sell except dreams.

Devoting so much editorial space to pieces unavailable for purchase was very risky, but the story paid off for *Vogue*, because >

< it reflected a zeitgeist. It acknowledged that mixing some old into your wardrobe looked new, and decreed that this was the mixed-up way modern women would dress in the brave new twenty-first century. This was *Vogue* at its most prescriptive, a throwback to the glorious Diana Vreeland regime. Trish Goff, the model featured in the story, loved the dresses so much that she bought every single one of them. Not a thing came back from that shoot.

Around the time that story ran in 2000, vintage transitioned from being something worn by quirky girls in goofy hats to serving as the red carpet anti-uniform for the most stylish starlets on the awards-show circuit. Actresses in the fashion vanguard, such as Winona Ryder and Demi Moore, opted to wear previously owned pieces to events rather than not-yet-produced runway samples. Photographers and fashion magazines, sick of the status quo, gravitated toward their decidedly non-commercial looks. People were fiending for something new, even if that something was old.

The next key break for Decades and vintage came in the wake of tragedy. Right after 9/11, a huge Renée Zellweger story ran in *Vogue*, and every single item she wore was vintage. Unlike Grace's editorial, this one was not planned. I was in Toronto at my friend Gina Gershon's movie premiere when the World Trade Center was attacked. I ended up stuck in Canada for several days,

and during my stay I got a call from Lisa Love, the West Coast editor of *Vogue*. She was absolutely frantic, telling me that all the current-season couture Renée was supposed to be wearing in the magazine had gotten caught up in customs because of 9/11, and there was nothing for her to wear.

Could I get hold of enough jaw-dropping pieces for the starlet, who was then at the peak of her career, to fill an entire story? It wasn't easy, but I did it. The photographs represented a triumph for everyone involved. In retrospect, vintage clothing was the closest thing to appropriate in the post-9/11 fashion climate, when conspicuous consumption became viewed as vulgar and even the most trend-hungry fashionistas turned inward for a while.

I've gotten a lot of notoriety from the famous women who wear Decades dresses to highly visible events. But just as important as these famous women are the not-always-so-famous women who provide the store with its incredible stock. The previous owner of a dress brings a certain life and spirit to a piece that imbues it with energy and dynamism. As hokey and New Age as this may sound, I really believe it: The spirit of the previous owner is crucial to the timeless appeal of a vintage dress. When a vintage dress has never been worn before, it seems sad in some way. Why do you think they call those dusty mountains of 1970s dungarees "dead stock"? Valuable as it may be, forgotten in

a warehouse and preserved to perfection, an unworn dress hasn't had its life yet —and I want my store to be full of life.

Scouting pieces for the store provides me with a wonderful opportunity to interact with women of different generations from my own—although the older I get, the smaller the age gap becomes between me and the women I buy from. These women welcome me into their homes—and, even more intimately, into their closets. I carry their tales with me long after their gowns have sold.

I remember one of the first women I bought from so clearly, I can still imagine myself back in the apartment with her. Her name was Marie, and she had recently lost her husband—the love of her life. For Marie, letting go of pieces from their time together was a way of honoring her late husband's place in her heart, and moving on with grace and respect. One of the first pieces I noticed when viewing Marie's collection was a black Chantilly lace and silk shift dress from the 1950s. It just had some magic to it. I looked up at Marie and smiled as I examined the dress, and she said, "Cameron, this is the dress I met my husband in."

Another buying experience I'll never forget came about all of a sudden when my partner, Jeff, and I were on vacation in Rome in 2006. A close friend and business associate e-mailed me to say that Irene Galitzine—the great Russian-born, Italian-bred princess of fashion

I love storytelling. I listen to every word my sellers tell me, and I proudly sell their stories along with their dresses.

design who invented palazzo pants—had passed away at the elegant age of ninety. I had always been an admirer of her style, so we contacted her estate to inquire about purchasing her archive.

I was amazed to be first in line: Apparently, her family hadn't really grasped the huge significance of what Princess Irene had done for fashion. I was exhilarated by the prospect of the clothes she left behind finding new lives with my clients. Princess Irene's family graciously allowed me and Jeff to visit her apartment, where we were honored to select pieces from her closets to be flown back to Los Angeles to find their new homes. It was such a privilege to be invited into this incredible woman's private world. I still feel a chill up my spine when I remember the impression her figure—enviable to the end—had left on her favorite chair. Its indentation was still there when we visited, even though her spirit had moved on.

Sometimes I work with a potential seller and realize she isn't quite ready to let go of something yet. When this happens, I never, ever push. In order for a gown to have a future, it has to be released into the world with love—"Fly free, little dress"—not spirited away under duress. Back in 1998, I visited with a woman who lived in the most incredible midcentury house in Beverly Hills, off Coldwater Canyon. After we spent a lovely afternoon reminiscing together, she was willing to part with armfuls of seventies

and eighties glamour, but my favorite piece in her collection—an incredible Thea Porter caftan—was her favorite piece as well. She just wasn't ready to say goodbye to it yet. Although it pained me to leave without that glorious item, I knew that this would not be the last time I'd see it.

More than twelve years later, this lady passed away at a wonderfully ripe old age. Hearing about her death, I remembered her fondly—and then I remembered that caftan. Believe it or not, her family recalled the way I felt about the dress, and allowed me to purchase it. I like to think this stylish lady would be quite pleased with her favorite caftan's new home in the Boston Museum of Fine Arts, to which it traveled after being worn by Julia Roberts in *Elle* magazine. Julia, who is a true Porter connoisseur, asked to buy the piece at her photo shoot, only to find that the object of her affection had already been promised to the MFA.

I'm interested not only in the personal interactions that arise out of my buying process, but also in the sociological observations I can make from what I buy and what I sell. I'm fascinated by what people are discarding and why, what people are consuming and why—and the relationship between the two. I'm utterly compelled by what our habits of fashion-collection say about our culture.

You can learn so much about a society from what it gets rid of. In our youth-obsessed

culture, middle-aged women might actually be afraid that owning and wearing incredible couture from years gone by will age them in the eyes of their peers. How wrong they are! I mean, which woman do you think looks older—a fifty-year-old wearing her daughter's skinny jeans, or that same woman in an elegant Bill Blass shift she wore the first time around in the 1980s? I've gone on home visits and told people, "Don't get rid of this yet. You can still wear it!"

I love storytelling. I listen to every word my sellers tell me, and I proudly sell their stories along with their dresses. Many people have expressed surprise that, given how close I get to each and every dress, I am able to let go of them so easily. I remind them that, first and foremost, Decades is a business. My goal is to sell things. And then I console them with the knowledge that while the dress leaves the premises, its story doesn't. I remember each and every tale. And soon I know the new story as well, because more often than not, the new owner will send me a picture of herself wearing whatever she's just bought.

Recently, at a museum benefit, I met a woman famous for discovering some of the most successful models of our time. Her job is to wander the cornfields of the Midwest looking for statuesque beauties who, although they likely don't know it, have the height, bone structure, and *je ne sais quoi* to sell millions of magazines. >

Fashion is a bit like quantum physics. Is a tastemaker identifying a moment, or creating it?

< This woman's name is Mary, and she is a scout. All Mary needs to do to know whether a girl can make it on the Paris runway is give her a quick glance as she walks around the mall.

A few weeks later, at a decidedly unglamorous vintage exposition in a nondescript municipal building in Santa Monica, California, I realized that I am the Mary of evening dresses. The friends I was with were constantly getting waylaid in the midst of racks and racks of—how can I say this?—*unspectacular* works of "fashion." They would hold up an anemic patterned shift, a limp black shirtwaist, a pile of pallid fur, and ask, with breathless insecurity, "This one? Do you like it? Do you think it's worth anything?" Over and over again, I rolled my eyes—as politely as I could, mind you—and dismissed each one. There was nothing to see here. Waste of a trip.

Then, on my way out of the convention center, I spotted a divine black velvet Halston gown draped over a mannequin whose ship had long since sailed. The dress was perfect. What was it still doing on the floor? The convention center doors had been open for three hours—every dealer in town must have seen it. It had to have been grossly overpriced, right? Wrong. Full of moth holes visible only close up? Nope. Pristine. I snapped it up for a song, my feelings alternating between guilt at possibly having taken advantage of a naive dealer, and

profound, elated superiority. Like a model scout, I have an ability to identify magic in things that other people just don't see. And I can kind of feel a moment, maybe before it's going to happen. Fashion is a little bit like quantum physics: Is a tastemaker identifying a moment, or creating it? It doesn't really matter. What matters is who's listening.

Technically, I no longer *have* to spend time on the sales floor. But I while away countless hours in the store with actresses and socialites, debutantes and bat mitzvah girls, wives and girlfriends, trying on dresses. Grace Jones and Ella Fitzgerald play in the background as the shoppers shyly peek out from the dressing room, anxious for an opinion. I love to be a matchmaker between a woman and her perfect dress. And making the right match seems so much more meaningful when the dress, like the woman, is one-of-a-kind.

That's what's incredible about vintage couture. There really is only one of something wonderful. Sometimes I'll buy a piece, and later discover a photograph of a woman wearing it twenty, thirty, even eighty years earlier. Not a photograph of a woman wearing a dress just like it, mind you—but wearing the same, actual dress itself.

My clients say that wearing these works of art, these sartorial artifacts, is magical. It's like becoming a piece of history. In our culture, sixteen-year-olds think nothing of buying a dress for $25.99, wearing it once,

then throwing it away—but I spend my life looking for fashion that deserves never to die. I am a sartorial vampire, scouring the globe for the most beautiful targets, then granting them eternal life.

"Style" is very easy to come by today. You can run to H&M or Zara and buy a very stylish outfit for less than you'll pay for the dinner you're wearing it to. For me and for my clients, though, just being stylish is not enough. The goal is to be singular and distinct—to wear something nobody has seen before. To have star quality. It's this sense of mystery that a truly rare item gives its owner, and it adds a certain allure: a power that can come only from wearing something whose provenance is not immediately identifiable.

When you think about it, nothing gets closer to a woman than her dress. It's enchanting, and quite humbling, really, to imagine all the places Decades gowns have been. A Decades gown travels with a woman, as the ultimate plus-one, on the most important nights of her life. And I like to think a little piece of me goes with it, cheering her on, too.

Anyone want to buy some illusions? I'm still selling.

The 1900s

Whether it's politics or hairstyles, each new century seems to spend its first decade shaking off the previous century's last. The ornate, formal fashions of the Edwardian period and the Belle Epoque carried straight through from the 1890s into the 1900s. The stiff corsetry and high collars worn across Europe and the States contorted women's bodies to resemble mannequins, and despite the pain, fashionable women delighted in the look.

Wealthy ladies spent countless hours planning their ensembles—even though many rarely left their homes—employing live-in ladies' maids to help them get dressed each day and evening. Every activity of daily living required a different outfit, and no dress was worth wearing unless one needed help getting into it.

Before party photos were easy to take, women from the very best families were immortalized in the paintings of John Singer Sargent, an American artist working in London. Sargent demonstrated an uncanny ability to evoke a subject's personality through expression, gaze, posture, and clothing, and soon found himself painting some of the world's most prominent social figures. An invitation to sit for Sargent became the hottest ticket in town.

The vision: tiny wasp waists, open necklines, and luxuriously waved tresses piled atop heads held just high enough to convey a touch of arrogance. Sargent's ladies were the chosen few, and they looked as though they knew it. The painter himself was a Svengali of sorts. He selected his subjects carefully, visited their homes, and chose their clothing and hairstyles. His works commanded about five thousand dollars in his day, equivalent to approximately one hundred thousand dollars now. Even though he was painting portraits, Sargent must have been aware that he was preserving—and prescribing—an archetypal image of womanhood, one that came to represent the look of his day.

While Sargent's portraits represented society's elite, the witty drawings of Charles Dana Gibson presented regular gals in all their glory. Gibson drew hundreds of lighthearted caricatures for popular magazines of the time, creating a populist archetype of the American woman at the turn of the century. Wearing the fashionable silhouette of the day—pigeon bosom, nipped-in waist, hobble skirt—the Gibson Girl was everywhere. She always appeared to have a twinkle in her eye, and naughty thoughts on her mind. Gibson's subjects seemed to have very modern, even powerful, spirits, conveyed by eyes almost brazen in their fearlessness to hold a gaze. In this way, the Gibson Girls were history's first pinups. They combined the restrictive, S-shaped silhouette of the late nineteenth century with a free and modern sense of public sensuality that was strictly twentieth.

Previous Detail of a gown made in the early 1900s. The vibrant peach fabric and contrasting silver embroidery come as a surprise, since we are so accustomed to seeing clothing from the Edwardian era in binary black and white.

Right Portrait of Anna Held, a Polish actress and singer who found fame in the United States as the partner and muse of nightlife mogul Florenz Ziegfeld. Ziegfeld reportedly paid her an astounding $1,500 per week to perform in his Broadway spectacles, so she had considerable discretionary income to spend on bespoke designer getups.

Far right Spectators at the 1908 horse races in Norderney, an island off the coast of Germany. Virginal white fabrics, big hats, and nipped-in waists epitomize the ultra-feminine Edwardian look.

Every activity required a different outfit, and no dress was worth wearing unless one needed help getting into it.

Previous, left John Singer Sargent's *Portrait of Madame X*, painted in 1884, was considered scandalous because of its overt sensuality. With her bare arms, neck, and décolletage, the subject is clearly an object of desire. Yet there is a strength in her hands, and in the way she looks defiantly away from the viewer—this woman is no wallflower.

Previous, right With her eighteen-inch waist and towering, pillowy hairdo, Camille Clifford, captured here in 1905, epitomizes the hourglass silhouette of the Gibson Girl.

Right John Waterhouse painted *My Sweet Rose* in 1908. Showing a woman in a state of ecstasy, but confined behind a brick wall, the painting can be read as an expression of repressed female sexuality.

Rose/Evelyn

The debate over standards of beauty in the 1900s was between the ideal and the real—essentially, between the painting and the photograph. Fashion, art, and even politics seemed to be asking one simple question: Was a woman most beautiful in her natural state or as refined by the rules of civility?

The range of images of women available to the public at the beginning of the twentieth century was broad. Fine art of the time—painting, specifically—focused on the flawless beauty of the feminine ideal. Paintings by the British artist John Waterhouse epitomized these fantasy women living in the hearts and minds of Victorians. Waterhouse's images of women, with their alabaster skin and Rapunzel hair, were inspired by art of the classical period. He engaged with themes taken up by the Romantics (read: beauty and death). Waterhouse frequently presented his subjects in serene states of self-reflection, subjugated to the gaze of the artist and the viewer, rarely making eye contact but very much in tune with their own sensuality. These were women as beautiful, mysterious flowers.

But at the same time that people were falling in love with Waterhouse's idealized women, new technology arrived on the scene: a machine that could immortalize the real. In February 1900, Kodak introduced its bestselling Brownie, the first point-and-shoot camera available to the public. All of a sudden, a photograph became an ephemeral document capturing a moment in time, rather than a serious artifact that needed to be planned, posed, and taken at a professional studio. Images could now be captured and circulated with relative ease and not much money. Now that life's more mundane moments could be captured on film, women began think about the way they dressed with a new awareness. Real people now became "personalities" because of the sudden availability and affordability of the camera.

The Gibson Girls, who existed in two dimensions simultaneously—in drawings and photographs, not to mention in "real" life—trained the public to make the connection between the real world and the world of representation. Where a "regular" woman likely couldn't identify with a Waterhouse or a Sargent subject, she could certainly see herself in a Gibson Girl. Charles Dana Gibson's illustrations were inspired by real women who had captured his attention. Many—such as his wife, the Southern belle Irene Langhorne—were socialites, but just as many were showgirls. The fact that these two distinct social types were represented in the same medium was an early indication of the democratization of beauty that would soon shake the twentieth century. >

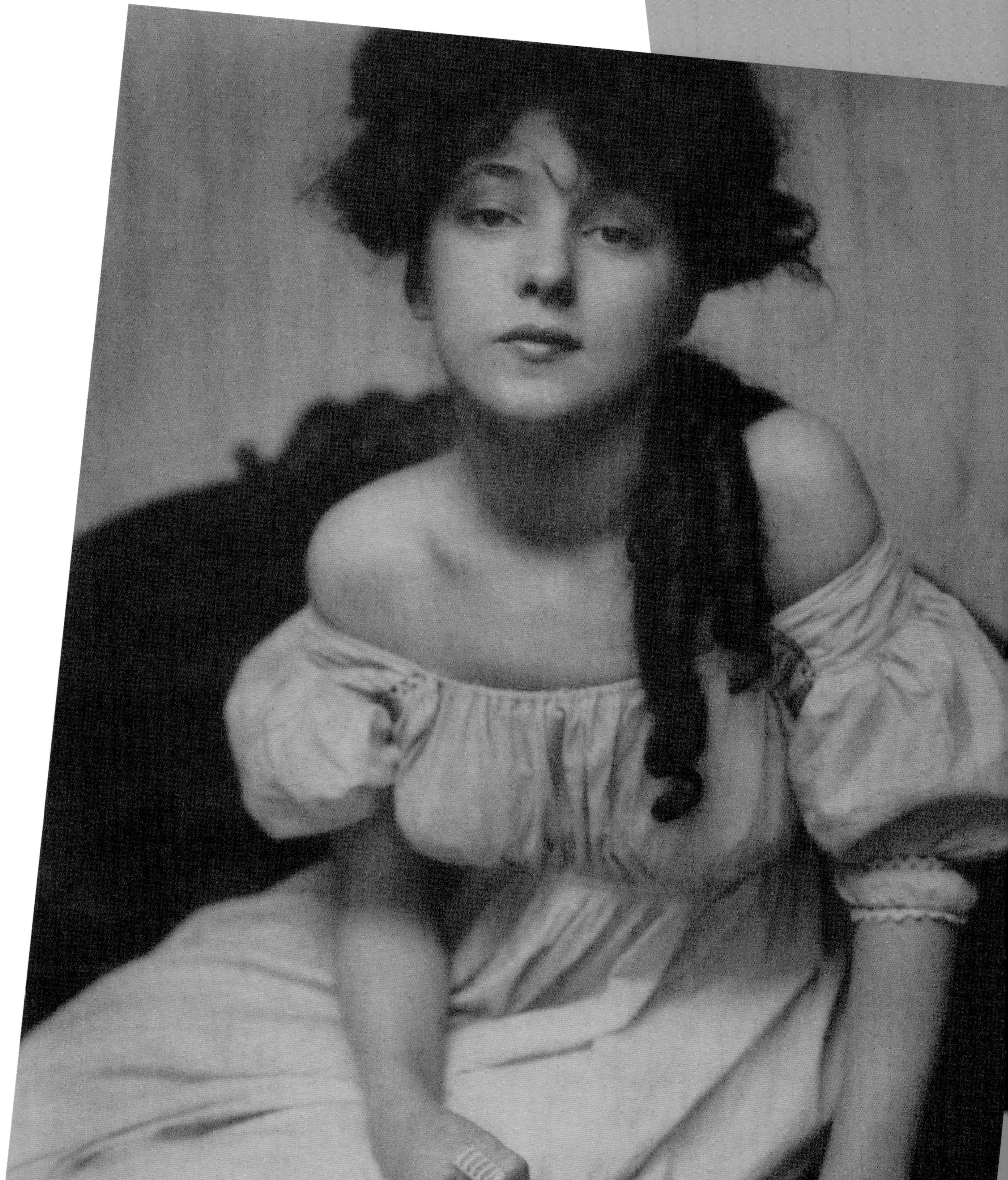

Nesbit was a classical beauty, with luxurious hair, skin like milk glass, lithe limbs, and a soft décolletage.

Evelyn Nesbit is just sixteen years old in this photograph, which Gertrude Käsebier shot in 1900. Her fearless confrontation of the lens and her bare shoulders convey an unbridled sensuality.

< Perhaps the most well-known Gibson Girl was Evelyn Nesbit. She famously appeared in 1903 on the cover of *Collier's* magazine, a national newsweekly, in profile, her hair styled to resemble a question mark. The drawing was titled *The Eternal Question*, and its inherent mystery suited the young woman whose allure would lead to the demise of the great architect Stanford White.

Nesbit's biography has the quality of an Edith Wharton novel. Her father, who was a struggling small-town lawyer, died before his time, leaving his wife and two young children saddled with debt. Evelyn, a ravishing beauty, kept food on the table by working as a model from the tender age of thirteen. Along with her mother and younger brother, she moved to New York City in the hopes of catching the eye of famous artists eager to capitalize on her youthful beauty. She was quickly discovered by the famous illustrator Gibson, and soon her face was plastered on the cover of every magazine in America. Then, at the age of sixteen, she was discovered in quite a different way by White, who was a world-renowned architect more than thirty years her senior. In exchange for her secret companionship, White moved Nesbit into a luxurious apartment and arranged to send her brother off to a prestigious military school. When Nesbit fell in love with the young actor John Barrymore, the jealous White whisked her away to a boarding

school, with her mother's approval. Finally free at the age of twenty, Nesbit married the wealthy industrialist Harry Thaw, in the hopes of starting a new life. Dining out one evening, the newlyweds ran into White. Thaw fired three shots into White's face, shouting either "You ruined my life" or "You ruined my wife" (to this day, no one can be sure which). Thaw was shipped off to the loony bin for life, and Nesbit, still just twenty-one, was disinherited by her uncaring mother-in-law and forced to earn her living doing vaudeville shows and waiting tables.

She was a classical beauty, with luxurious hair that fell past her waist, skin like milk glass, lithe limbs, and a soft décolletage. But the most captivating thing about Nesbit was her willingness to connect with the camera, the sheer sexiness of her gaze. Her self-possessed yet vulnerable beauty transcended the period from whence she came.

Nesbit typically posed in dresses that had minimal structure, coverage, or adornment— garments that were precisely opposite to the painfully articulated, highly ornamented styles fashionable among the elite of the day. Nesbit's gowns were usually light in color, with easygoing, elasticized, off-the-shoulder sleeves and low, wide necklines. Despite always being fully clothed in photographs, Nesbit seems to exist almost in a state of nakedness, her clothes attempting to crawl

off her body. She appears to be proud of her skin rather than ashamed of it, as would have been expected of a woman living in her times.

Nesbit's straightforward beauty sent a clear message to all the fancy ladies inhabiting the well-appointed drawing rooms of New York, London, and Paris: No longer would yards of taffeta covered in jewels and feathers render a gal worthy of a second look. Now, in order to be truly captivating, a woman had to have a special something she simply could not buy. Star quality and natural radiance trumped silk, makeup, and jewels once society entered the age of the photograph. Black-and-white imagery could reduce the impact of expensive clothing, but it could not stifle the appeal of an extraordinarily beautiful girl.

Nesbit was the sort of spirited beauty who could show up at an event wearing a dress costing less than most other women's stockings and capture the attention of every man in the room. When she appeared in a photograph wearing no more than a cotton gown worth a few dollars, she still looked like a million bucks.

When it came to looking current, wealthy women spared no expense. In 1900, just as for the last third of the previous century, the House of Worth weaved the label for which affluent women lusted. Representing the ultimate in couture glamour, Worth was the first fashion house to sew branded labels into made-to-order items, and also the first to present collections to clients via runway shows.

Although the house's founder, Charles Frederick Worth, was British, he was widely considered to be the father of Paris couture. Worth the man was as famous as his label and his ensembles can be found throughout society portraiture from the turn of the century. No longer was it enough to have a beautiful dress sewn just for you from the finest of materials—now it needed to bear the mark of the aptly named House of Worth.

Made-to-order from start to finish, dresses from Worth were unconscionably expensive, especially considering that many were crafted from such delicate fabric and adorned with such perishable trims that they could be worn only once. No wonder a debutante dressed in Worth was under enormous pressure to snag a rich husband. Who knew whether her family could ever afford to dress her so well again?

Meanwhile, the design collective Callot Soeurs—which was also based in Paris—is credited with introducing the world of couture to some of the Eastern influences that would soon take it by storm. It brought metallic fabrics, jewels, kimono sleeves, and harem pants from Marrakech and Shanghai to Paris and London, opening haute couture's eyes to the new cultural trend in Orientalism.

Formed in 1895 by the four Callot sisters, who were born into the Parisian lace trade, Callot Soeurs was famous for its intensely decorated evening gowns, coats, and capes partly inspired by the extravagant fashions of eighteenth-century France. This aesthetic was on the opposite end of the spectrum from someone like Evelyn Nesbit's modern, easygoing glamour.

Designs by Callot Soeurs were impeccably constructed and highly structured. Madeleine Vionnet, the legendary couturier who rose to prominence in the 1910s (see page 38), was trained by the sisters and always credited her dressmaking virtuosity to their teaching methods. It was while working for them, she said, that she learned to drape fabric directly on the body, instead of cutting it on a table.

Unlike Callot Soeurs, which preserved structural tradition with restrictive corsets and S-shaped silhouettes, the singular designer Jeanne Paquin prided herself on breaking from it. The first woman ever to establish her own couture house, in 1891, Paquin lived her dream like a Belle Epoque Diane von Furstenberg, moving through public life as her own best advertisement. Invited to showcase her designs at Paris's Universal Exhibition in 1900, Paquin commissioned a wax replica of herself, then dressed it in her designs, rather than hiring a model who might not have precisely the right look. While her pieces were impeccably sewn and intricately adorned, starting in 1905 she began to relax the conventional S-shape silhouette—allowing women's bodies to relax as well.

Dressmakers/Tastemakers

Overleaf, left Photographed in Italy, this unstructured, strapless gown from 1902 marks a major departure from the severe, uncomfortable styles of the previous century.

Overleaf, right Actress Elizabeth Firth as countess-slash-lion-tamer Olga, in a musical from 1909 called *The Dollar Princess.* Her adventurous headdress reflects the exoticism that was coming into vogue.

Left A wealthy client stands patiently during her fitting at the House of Worth in 1907. Instead of shopping at a department store, or asking a dressmaker to create one-of-a-kind looks, fashionable women at the turn of the last century chose from a selection of sample styles, then commissioned made-to-order ensembles.

DESIGNER OF THE DECADE

Paul Poiret

Even though it is widely acknowledged that Jeanne Paquin is the designer who freed women from their S-shaped prisons, the man who often gets credit is Paul Poiret. Responsible for dressing high society's hard-partying set at the turn of the century, he created an easy, free-flowing silhouette that echoed women's increasing freedom in society. Having learned dressmaking at Parisian couturiers Doucet and the House of Worth, Poiret had the pedigree, the knowledge, and the ego to change fashion. Unlike political progressives who espoused dowdiness as the key to women's liberation, Poiret believed he could make women both comfortable and beautiful at the same time, by raising the waistline of his patterns and allowing the body of a dress to float straight down from below the breasts.

Poiret began sewing as a small child. Legend has it that when his sisters gave him a wooden doll to play with, he squirreled away a pile of scraps from his family's umbrella factory, then immediately set to work dressing that little doll like a proper lady.

He made his name when the famous Parisian actress Réjane commissioned a coat from the House of Doucet in 1898, while he was still working there. When Poiret left Doucet to start his own house, Réjane followed him. The popular actress appeared all over town in Poiret's lavish designs, and

as other women strove to emulate her look, his business thrived. In 1905 he married the gorgeous Denise Boulet, a fine-featured, vaguely exotic brunette who became his lifelong muse. It was she who inspired the high-waisted, corsetless line Poiret referred to as "Directoire" in 1906.

When asked to trace the evolution of his aesthetic, Poiret explained that when his wife was a young mother, she was too busy to bother with intricate foundation garments. It was in response to Denise's need that he came up with his best work. For Poiret to publicly draw a direct connection between his personal life and his designs was a brilliant public relations move, one that designers have been copying ever since.

Denise was photographed frequently and women aspired to be like her. The Poirets held exclusive parties in their luxurious garden, which was protected by a custom-made inflatable canopy when it rained so as not to ruin the revelry. At these soirées, the couple showcased Poiret's exquisite eye and Denise's exquisite beauty. Not long after launching his clothing business, Poiret created the world's first designer fragrance, and even ventured into the world of interior decoration, making his the original lifestyle brand.

At the height of his success, Poiret sported a fanciful turban over his long hair, and traveled with an entourage of Russian ballet dancers, whom he dressed like one another around a theme, according to his whim. >

A group of stylish women wearing Poiret in 1910. The Japanese-style parasols they carry are evidence of the influence that Orientalism had on Poiret's designs. In the United States, Poiret became known as "The King of Fashion," while in his hometown of Paris he was called "Le Magnifique."

< Rather than asking women what they might like to wear, he was quite comfortable telling them what they ought to wear, with an almost despotic vigor. Poiret made the trend in exoticism accessible, encouraging a playful mystery—a spirit of wanderlust—in the clothing he designed, as well as in his highly publicized lifestyle. His easy-fitting silhouettes, jewel tones, metallic accents, and pajamas for evening conjured up the glamour of a faraway world, once reachable only by camel. As much as Poiret strove to simplify women's undergarments, working for decades in an effort to make the corset extinct, he took every opportunity to embellish their outer garments. Patterned fabrics were designed by the most important artists of the day. Tights that were once black became red, purple, or gold. Slippers were bejeweled. Jackets were trimmed in fur.

Poiret used his own covetable lifestyle to build a reputation that transcended categories, and ultimately, his celebrity became as important as his designs. The Poirets would have given Studio 54's Steve Rubell a run for his money: Among their wild guests, body jewelry was not uncommon, and rumor has it that those zany Poirets allowed birds and monkeys to roam free at their celebrations. Much later, in the 1970s, when the rich and beautiful made pilgrimages to places like Marrakech in search of beauty and adventure, they were no doubt tipping their turbans to Monsieur Poiret.

Right Irish actress and singer Daisy Irving, star of *The Count of Luxembourg*, a musical play, in 1910. She wears a lampshade dress designed by Paul Poiret, one of the first styles that rendered complicated, structured undergarments obsolete.

Far right Paul Poiret styling a model in his Paris studio. Instead of getting mired in menial tasks such as pinning garments himself, Poiret chose to stand back and take in the big picture.

Poiret's easy-fitting silhouettes, jewel tones, metallic accents, and pajamas for evening conjured up the glamour of a faraway world, once reachable only by camel.

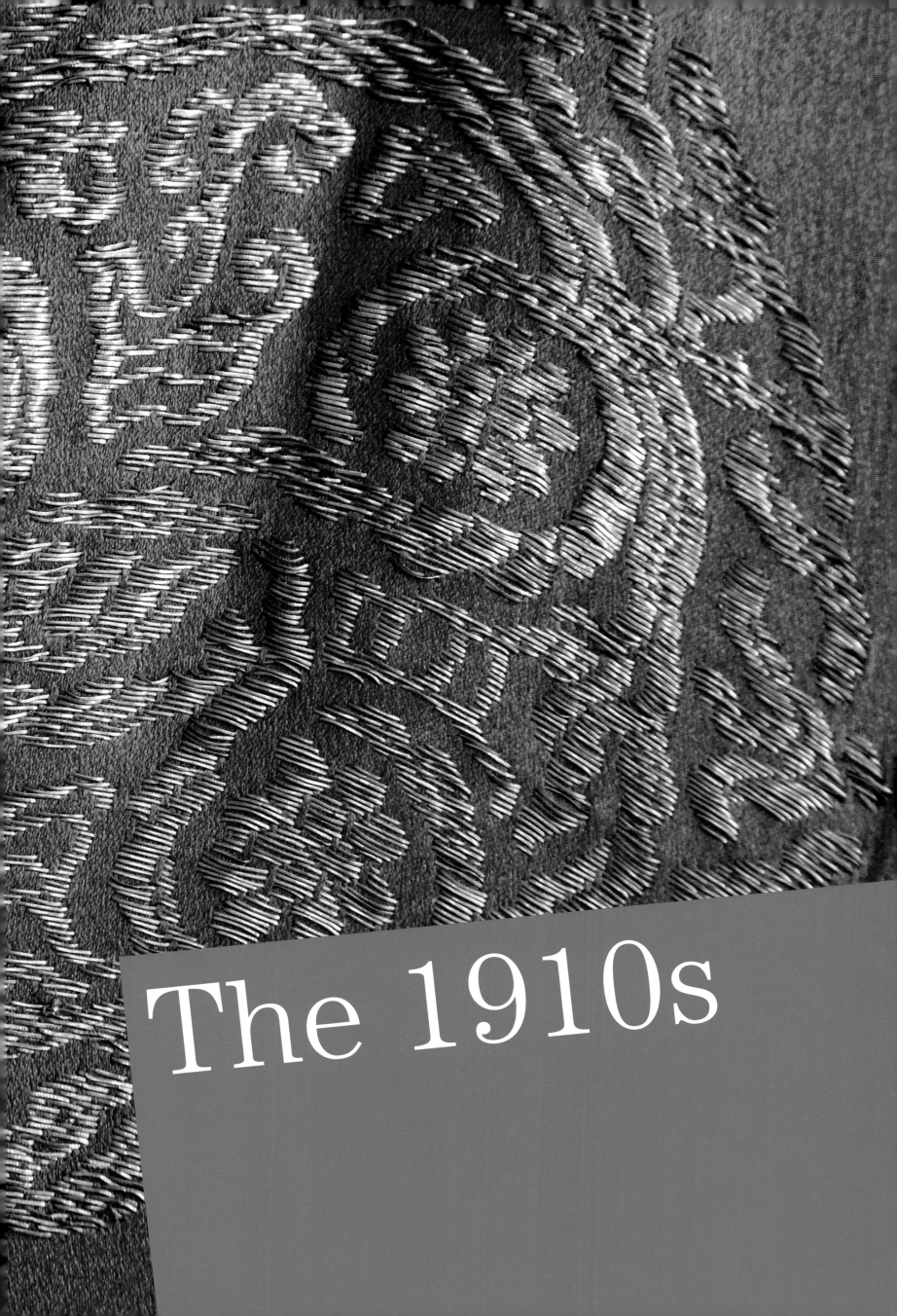

The 1910s

The second decade of the twentieth century really began in 1914, with the First World War. The trauma and trials of war transformed the flamboyant designer Paul Poiret into a modest tailor and replaced the fashion world's glorious silk confections with functional jersey sheaths. With strict fabric rationing and a dearth of labor, the couture industry was effectively brought to a halt. Because the ultra-high-end market was virtually eliminated, fashion continued its shift from displaying ostentatious ornamentation to emphasizing shape—a transition that had already been set in motion by Jeanne Paquin and Poiret during the previous decade.

Although Poiret had previously been at the vanguard, his work took a giant—or rather small, actually—step backward. In 1910, he introduced the hobble skirt, a bizarrely confining garment that bound the knees close together, forcing the woman wearing it to take tiny, awkward steps. Stylish American lady Edith Russell was wearing a hobble skirt on board the *Titanic* in 1912, and it almost cost her her life. "I'm a prisoner in my own skirt," she told other passengers, "I can't even walk, much less jump across the ocean into a lifeboat." Needless to say, despite her skirt, she survived the disaster and lived to tell the tale—no thanks to the punishing creation of Monsieur Poiret.

By and large, in the 1910s, women abandoned highly structured designs in favor of fluidity. Where progressive design once strove simply not to limit the body's movement, it now aimed to encourage it, from modern-dance-inspired gowns that were designed in homage to classical statuary, to proto-flapper sheaths that were tailored to swing along to the music. The brassiere, invented in 1912, brought a new freedom to even the modest, and no one, no matter what her preferred style of dance, complained. With such a wide variety of new silhouettes and trends, the one constant in the 1910s was clothing that celebrated the body's movement, rather than constraining it. With limited resources and newly relaxed social conventions, the body, rather than the clothes covering (or not covering) it, became the star of the show.

Previous Detail of a kimono-style belted dress in raspberry red, embroidered with gold, by Vitaldi Babani. He offered original, Eastern-inspired creations, as well as collaborating with Fortuny and Liberty of London.

Right Captured by Jugendstil photographer Jacob Hilsdorf, these young women's prim yet romantic look was emblematic of the period just before the First World War (Jugendstil was essentially the German interpretation of Art Nouveau).

Overleaf, left Gustav Klimt's *Portrait of Johanna Staude*, begun in 1918, was found unfinished after the Viennese artist's death. The vibrant, block-print pattern on Staude's coat was designed by Martha Alber, a member of the Austrian avant-garde Arts and Crafts collective Wiener Werkstätte.

Overleaf, right Reclining in her Paris apartment, singer and actress Régine Flory wears a Fortuny design from 1910. Unafraid of controversy and innuendo, Flory was notorious for her seductive musical theater routines—and attitude.

The body, rather than the clothes, became the star of the show.

Both before and after the war was on, stylish women of the 1910s expressed themselves with their bodies. Until now, allowing one's body to be truly seen, even in silhouette, verged on profane. But with society in crisis and social rules relaxing, the movement in fashion was toward freedom.

Isadora Duncan was the godmother of modern dance. After a bohemian upbringing in Northern California, she moved to Europe with a theater troupe and ended up in Paris. A barefoot vision who wore togas inspired by Classical Greece or long dresses almost childlike in their simplicity, Duncan broke all the rules of traditional dance, as well as the rules of traditional dressing. Instead of being piled ornately atop her head, her long hair was parted and gathered sedately, or left to hang wavy and loose. Her body was unadorned. In contrast to the uncomfortable, subjugated look of women in corsets or hobble skirts, Duncan's loose, unstudied freedom evoked the ultimate form of classical feminine beauty.

A fashion designer directly inspired by Duncan was Madeleine Vionnet, who founded her own house in Paris in 1912 after training with Callot Soeurs (see page 25) and Jacques Doucet. Like Duncan, Vionnet was obsessed with antiquity, taking inspiration from the styles of drapery shown on Greek and Roman statuary. Vionnet believed that a woman's movement should not be constricted by

her clothing, and she is widely credited with discovering the bias cut, a method of cutting fabric that could transform a simple dress from sacklike to curve-skimming—no boning required.

Vionnet worked in a labor-intensive and bizarrely charming manner. She draped a miniature version of each dress on a toddler-size yet adult-proportioned doll mounted atop a piano bench. Once she had placed every fold and cascade where she wanted it, she executed the dress again, in average human size.

Martha Graham was another choreographer and dancer whose reach extended far beyond the world of dance. Even though she was raised in a conventional Protestant home, Graham invented a movement language that seemed positively ecstatic—and not in a religious way. When choosing what to wear for her performances, Graham favored diaphanous gowns to show off her lithe physique. The creations of Mariano Fortuny y Madrazo, a Spanish designer who was Graham's frequent collaborator, expressed both the earthy corporeality and the goddess-like spirit of modern dance. >

Isadora/Irene

Left Members of American ex-pat
Isadora Duncan's dance troupe,
"The Isadorables," gather by a
window at her school in Germany.

Above Isadora Duncan reclines
on a daybed in her Berlin studio
in 1914. Duncan's philosophy of
fashion was much the same as
her philosophy of dance: natural,
unencumbered, and free.

With gowns that were both closely fitted and demure, Castle cut an intriguing figure.

Previous, left Ballroom dancer Irene Castle with two of her pets, Brussels Griffon dogs Joseph and Moomee, in the early 1910s. An animal advocate, Castle founded a shelter called Orphans of the Storm just outside Chicago.

Previous, right Ultimate It Couple Irene and Vernon Castle in around 1913. Vernon died just four years later. The book Irene wrote about their life together, *My Husband*, was made into a film starring Ginger Rogers and Fred Astaire in 1939.

Left Irene Castle posing with a fan made of feathers in New York in 1918. Along with her husband, Vernon, Castle helped start the foxtrot craze when she performed the dance in a Broadway play called *Watch Your Step*, by the then-unknown Irving Berlin.

< More a textile artist than a dressmaker, Fortuny excelled at creating new pleating and printing techniques on silk. His signature pleating style was to allow fabric to fall in uniform folds as thin as ribbons, whose combination of fluidity and geometry created an effect reminiscent of the robes of ancient Greece. Fortuny named his two most famous pieces, the Knossos scarf and the Delphos gown, in a nod to the culture that inspired him. Flowing straight to the floor from the shoulders, the Delphos was ultrabasic in its cut but revolutionary in its freedom of shape. The narrow, precise pleats Fortuny added to this essentially shapeless silhouette gave it a sense of refinement and polish.

But it was a ballroom dancer—not a modern one—who had the most modern look of all. The elegant brunette Irene Castle found fame, along with her husband, Vernon, as half of the world's most famous dancing duo. Barely out of her teens when she began performing, Castle became something of a fashion idol almost immediately. Whippet-thin, she bobbed her hair in 1914 in preparation for a hospital stay to have her appendix removed, because she couldn't stand the feeling of other people combing her hair. Soon, perfectly healthy women all over the country were following suit. One estimate is that within a week, hundreds of fans had bobbed their hair; within a couple of weeks, thousands. Having short hair, which became the dominant fashion in the 1920s and '30s,

was still positively rebellious in 1914. But the trend caught on, perhaps because it conveyed both the feeling of austerity brought on by the war and a new feminine freedom.

With gowns that were both closely fitted and demure, that hinted at her shape without revealing it entirely, Castle cut an intriguing figure. While Duncan and Graham had a dramatic, classical vibe that was overwrought, highly expressive, and mature in its womanliness, Castle's gamine silhouette and quick and agile performances of her signature dance—the foxtrot—gave her an easygoing, almost tomboyish appeal.

Exotic/Erotic

Right With her feathered headdress and skirt, Denise Poiret is ahead of the flock as she poses in a look from her husband Paul's 1919 collection. Behind her is Constantin Brancusi's celebrated Modernist sculpture, *Bird*.

Overleaf, left Mata Hari, the Dutch spy, displaying her formidable collection of body jewelry in 1914. The exotic dancer was captured by the French in 1917, and later executed by firing squad, charged with spying for Germany during the First World War. Her adopted name comes from the word "sun" in Indonesian—she picked it up while living as an officer's wife in the Dutch East Indies.

Overleaf, right Actress Theda Bara dressed as Salome in the 1918 film of the same name. The *New York Times* described her as "every minute the vampire, in manner and movement and expression." Any woman willing to show this much skin was dangerous, plain and simple.

It was a traveling ballet company from Russia that ignited an Orientalist obsession all over the United States and Europe. Known for collaborating with avant-garde artists of the time, the Ballets Russes brought a total visual experience to its patrons, from posters to programs, costumes to stage sets. The company's most influential costume designer was Léon Bakst, who created looks for many ballets, including the company's first hit, *Cleopatra*, in 1909, and *Scheherazade*, in 1910.

In addition to all the glitz and jewel tones one would expect in a Russian interpretation of Oriental costume, the getups in these ballets were revolutionary in the fact that they freed the torsos of the women who wore them. Now middles were not only unconstrained but also exposed. Female dancers wore bras and hip belts to conceal their lady parts, but everything else was either left bare or covered in a diaphanous fabric that moved with the body and skimmed its surface, inviting the audience to gaze freely upon the dancers' undulating bodies. Monsieur and Madame Poiret (see page 28) were, of course, preeminent patrons and rabid fans of the Ballets Russes, and many of Poiret's designs were heavily influenced by their costumes.

Another designer with an Eastern fascination was Jeanne Lanvin, who started her couture house in 1909, when stylish women began to inquire whether the dresses she made for her young daughter came in adult sizes. It was precisely their childlike quality—fantastical ornamentation, rich color, simple silhouettes—that made Lanvin's pieces stand out in both the highly structured period before the war and the austere days of wartime. In the 1920s, Lanvin would be one of the first to dress legions of flappers—rich party girls—in highly ornamented but barely structured chemises.

The Orientalist craze didn't only produce fashion. It also provided a convenient loophole in the social code that allowed ladylike actresses to masquerade as brazen. Actresses who put on make-believe exotic identities found mainstream fame by mystifying, intriguing, and titillating their public. No longer did women need to be elegant, proper, and appropriate—provided they spoke with an accent, of course. These new personalities could take the same overt sexuality the Russian dancers exhibited onstage and use it to craft a persona of musk-scented mystery.

Theda Bara, a silent film actress, cultivated a dark and predatory image that conflated the archetypes of the vampire and the femme fatale. The roles that she played associated exoticism with a sexy brand of danger. As the lead part in the 1917 hit movie *Cleopatra*, with costumes designed by George Hopkins, she wore sooty kohl eyeliner and lipstick so dark it was nearly black, which made her look as though she'd painted her face with blood. Her gowns, at once ethereal and somber, were sheer enough to make the viewer wonder whether she was wearing any undergarments. As for her personal life, Bara had a pet snake and traveled in a white limousine with male attendants dressed as Nubian slaves. Born Theodosia Goodman in 1885, Bara didn't come from the far-off reaches of the Orient, but rather from Cincinnati, Ohio. Her willful projection of a dangerous, overt, poisonous sexuality—the allure of a temptress who aims to kill with pleasure—foreshadowed a powerful trend that has been present in every decade since.

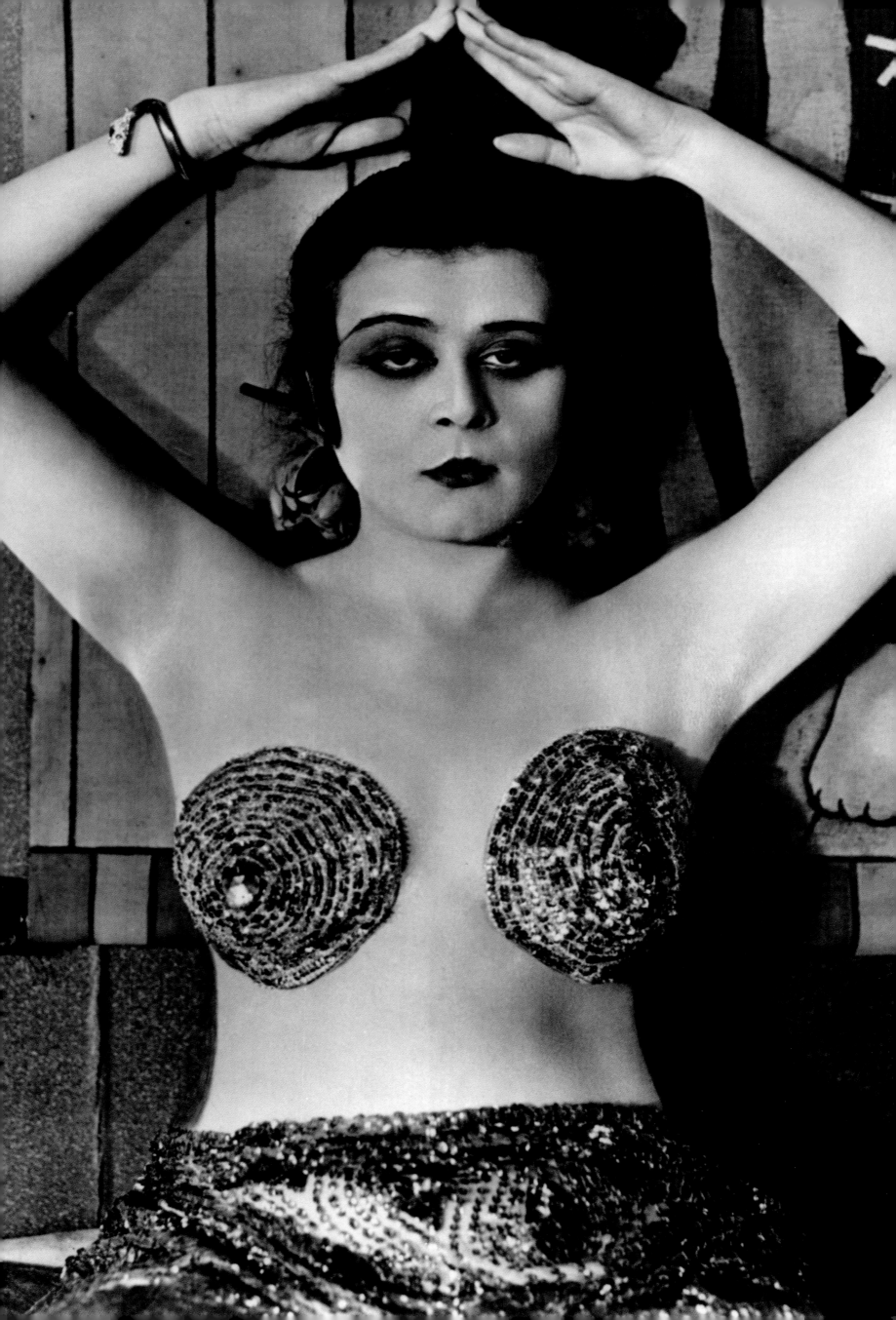

DESIGNER OF THE DECADE

Lucile

Lucile, a.k.a. Lady Duff Gordon, a.k.a. Lucy Sutherland, is sometimes credited with designing the world's first brassiere, in 1912, but she was also responsible for bringing the intimacy, delicacy, and intricate handwork of lingerie to street clothes, pioneering the concept of underwear as outerwear.

Like many fashion legends, she had begun sewing out of necessity, in order to support her young daughter after her divorce. Soon, her unconventionally unstructured undergarments and tea gowns—the Belle Epoque's version of the housecoat—were in demand, and "Lucile," as her label was known, was opening stores all over the world.

With a knack for branding and marketing, the designer named her dresses after what had inspired them. Among these "gowns of emotion" were confections called "The Sighing Sound of Lips Unsatisfied" and "A Frenzied Song of Amorous Things." Lucile's gowns brought with them a world of fantastical associations. She produced major runway shows, with live music, beautiful models, and an impermeable velvet rope. Lucile dressed most It Girls of the day, among them Irene Castle (see page 43) and the young American superstar Mary Pickford, and she signed endorsement deals for everything from shoes to limousines.

Lucile, as both a label and a persona, offered a preview of the increased freedom and autonomy women would find in the 1920s as the fashion industry gained importance in modern society. Most well-heeled American women had long been happy to procure their wardrobes from their local dressmakers, who would tailor getups according to their clients' specifications, with perhaps a vague awareness of what was going on stylistically in Europe. But by the second decade of the twentieth century, as designers' personae became as important as their designs, women thousands of miles from Paris had been bit by the designer fashion bug, and labels—not just the confections they produced—had begun to matter.

Above British dancer Florence Walton poses for the camera in 1915, wearing a creation by Lucile. The wildly popular designer named all her gowns, and this hooped crinoline creation was fittingly called "Youth."

Right A model wears a pale off-the-shoulder dress by Lucile (along with a come-hither stare). The ethereal, easygoing style seems unstructured, but all Lucile's designs actually featured intricate undercarriages.

The 1920s

Flappers were the original punks. First of all, consider the hair. Punks had mohawks; flappers had bobs. Opting for an elegant little chin-length do may not seem all that rebellious nowadays, but in a time when a woman's mop was considered her crowning glory, back when whores and beggars exchanged their ponytails for food money only when teetering on the edge of starvation, a girl who chose to look like a little Dutch boy was making a serious statement.

Second, the clothes. The message sent by leather and denim in the late seventies was the same as that of the straight, knee-length chemises in the early twenties: one of confident androgyny. Like flappers, punk girls wanted to be seen to be as freewheeling as boys, unlimited by society's preconceived notions of the "weaker" gender. Neither wanted to be categorized purely as a function of their secondary sex characteristics.

But third, and most important, was the lifestyle. Both punks and flappers blew big, wet raspberries in the face of the establishment. Whether it was sex, drugs, and the Charleston, or sex, drugs, and rock 'n' roll, these teens and twentysomethings were at the vanguard of the counterculture. Both indulged in illegal drugs: the punks, in everything from alcohol to cocaine, and the flappers,

in everything from cocaine to . . . alcohol. Back then, of course, alcohol was illegal in the United States. In subsequent decades, their "bizarre" and disobedient behavior would set the mainstream standard.

Both flappers and punks defined their aesthetics by attitude, becoming iconic as much for what they represented as for what they looked like. In the first two decades of the twentieth century, the Gibson Girls had tantalized the American imagination with their Rapunzel locks, teardrop breasts, tiny waists, and soft shoulders. But after the First World War, women started stripping down to their basic attributes—some literally—whittling away everything nonessential until only their wispy bodies remained.

Not everyone "got" the whole flapper thing immediately. An article in a 1920 edition of the *Atlantic Monthly* called attention to the generational divide in attitude toward the flapper culture:

Flappers trot like foxes, limp like lame ducks, one-step like cripples, and all to the barbaric yawp of strange instruments which transform the whole scene into a moving-picture of a fancy ball in Bedlam.

This sentence could describe virtually any youth counterculture scene that's emerged in the years since it was written.

Cultural critics have theorized ad nauseum about why the flappers made such a splash.

"It was the explosion of assembly-line manufacturing," some said. "These girls wanted to be sleek, fast, and efficient like machines," surmised others. "Dowdy schoolmarms won the right to vote with their minds—and now their daughters were going to vote with their bodies," posited still others. Probably the most widely accepted historical viewpoint is that the trauma of the First World War had shocked Young America— and Young Europe, too—into throwing all caution to the wind. They either felt invincible for surviving it or had become so quickly acquainted with death that they wanted to live at maximum volume, for fear their lives would be cut as short as their hair. Probably all these factors, and dozens more, made an impact. But—as they would again in the late 1970s—politics, hormones, and inspiration combined to change the way fashion looked forever.

Previous Detail of a vibrant salmon, deep red, and pearly pink sequined fishtail dress by Paul Poiret, from around 1925. Made just four years before the shuttering of the House of Poiret, this ornately decorated piece reflects the brilliance of the Roaring Twenties.

Right Dorothy Sebastian, Joan Crawford, and Anita Page in *Our Dancing Daughters*, a film from 1928. Although Crawford found fame as a serious actress, she started out as just another dancing girl.

Far right An actress in one of the Mack Sennett comedies dances the Charleston in 1925. Although it probably had an Afro-American origin, the dance was most popular among young Caucasian rebels.

Overleaf, left Marion Morehouse— a.k.a. Mrs. e e cummings—posing for Edward Steichen in 1926. She wears a moiré gown with a plunging back and huge bow, designed by Louise Boulanger.

Overleaf, right From 1924, another collaboration between Marion Morehouse and Edward Steichen— this time with a gown by Chanel.

The iconic look of the 1920s girl has endured as one of the most sophisticated of all time.

Josephine/Zelda

Perhaps the 1920s wasn't the first decade in which the young and decadent were acting up, but it was the first decade when the whole country knew about it. In the twenties, the public gained access to the personal lives of the celebrities and public figures who fascinated them. No longer satisfied by knowing what an actress wore in a film, her fans also wanted to know what that same actress dressed in on her days off. Socialites such as Zelda Fitzgerald were photographed at both debutante balls and more quotidian times: setting sail on a steamer ship, three sheets to the wind at a speakeasy. Because photographic equipment had become even more portable by 1920 than it had been just a few years before, the everyday moments of the rich and famous were recorded, and regular folk could peer into the lives of the beautiful people. No longer did a handful of meticulously staged photographs represent a stylish woman's image to the public—now the world had access to her real-life lifestyle.

Two other technological breakthroughs that fed the flapper culture were the sound film and the portable record player. In 1927, *The Jazz Singer* became the first feature-length sound film in wide release. With the record player, now people all over the world could hear real, "live" jazz captured in Harlem or Paris, right there in the comfort of their own homes. Once-quiet drawing rooms brimmed over with sweaty young bodies practicing the dance craze du jour.

Unlike the punk aesthetic of later youth counterculture, the iconic look of the 1920s girl has endured as one of the most sophisticated of all time, probably because the straightforward silhouette of the flapper dress put the spotlight on the young body, and the bobbed hair put the spotlight on the young face. Personality and natural beauty, rather than wealth and artifice, were now the key to a woman's appeal.

Zelda Fitzgerald and Josephine Baker are each regarded as quintessential flappers, but they represent opposite sides of the craze: One was an aristocrat; the other, an outsider.

Fitzgerald, née Sayre, was the debutante wife of F. Scott, the world-renowned writer. Born in 1900 to a wealthy Southern family, Zelda was the original girl-gone-wild, and she knew every single rule to break. Her all-American, golden-haired, light-eyed beauty was timeless, but her wavy bob, boyish riding clothes, and sassy joie de vivre were quintessentially-of-the-moment. Although Zelda was anti-artifice, she was admired for her looks by both men and women alike. >

The ultimate flapper posing on a tiger rug in 1925. Although the world was smitten with her, Josephine Baker maintained a down-to-earth modesty when it came to her looks: "Beautiful? It's all a question of luck. I was born with good legs. As for the rest . . . beautiful, no. Amusing, yes."

Zelda was highly athletic, a daredevil, and aware of her feminine power from a young age.

Left The soon-to-be Mrs. F. Scott Fitzgerald seated on a flower bed, in costume for a production of *Folly*, in 1919. Demure in this photograph, Zelda was known to be quite a handful. When she got wind that rumors were circulating about her fondness for swimming naked, she began wearing a nude-colored suit just to encourage them.

Right This ballet-inspired tea gown was shockingly low-cut for its time—but not for Josephine Baker. She was known for her revealing getups. Speaking of her heyday style, she once said, "I wasn't really naked. I simply didn't have any clothes on."

< Zelda was known as a rebel in Montgomery, Alabama, where she grew up: highly athletic, a daredevil, and aware of her feminine power from a young age. Her friend Eleanor Addison once reflected,

When she commandeered a streetcar bright and early one Sunday morning and went clanging down Court Street with the befuddled motorman practically hanging on the ropes, the town criers lifted their eyes to the heavens and said "disgraceful." When she danced like an angel in a pink ballet costume at some charity affair, the same town criers mumbled, "beautiful."

Zelda and Scott Fitzgerald had a tumultuous marriage, and their fortune varied wildly according to Scott's publishing deals and alcohol consumption. But they spent the better part of the decade frolicking with the world's most interesting people, from Hemingway to Picasso. In 1922, Zelda published what many considered to be an autobiographical story in *Metropolitan* magazine, titled, "Eulogy on the Flapper."

The Flapper awoke from her lethargy . . . bobbed her hair, put on her choicest pair of earrings and a great deal of audacity and rouge and went into the battle. She flirted because it was fun to flirt and wore a one-piece bathing suit because she had a good figure . . . She was conscious that the things she did were the things she had always wanted to do. Mothers disapproved of their sons taking the Flapper to dances, to teas, to swim and most of all to heart.

Zelda had come to represent the iconic flapper in the American cultural consciousness, but at the age of twenty-two, when most women were just starting to emulate the style of wild American party girls, the trendsetting Zelda Fitzgerald was moving on. Perhaps her heart had already set sail for Paris, where the Fitzgeralds would relocate in 1924.

Josephine Baker, another American who left for Paris, was a woman of color whose self-aware "exotic" routine came to represent the Harlem Renaissance. She found both her fame and her second home in France, which offered her more freedom and dignity than did the United States. Paris in the 1920s boasted a thriving African-American expatriate community, in great part because of the States' racist climate. The twenties, of course, were known as the Jazz Age, and nowhere was the jazz swinging like it was in the bars of Paris, where African-American entertainers met with less prejudice than they encountered at home.

The French called the style of music that Americans brought to Montmartre "Le Jazz Hot," and the men playing it on the Right Bank were largely members of the Harlem Hellfighters, a regiment that remained in Europe after the fighting of the First World War ended. Their nightlife colony boasted few women, but its queen was Josephine Baker. She was the ultimate showgirl, appearing in costumes grand and wacky enough to be worn on a Vegas stage today. She "trained" at the Folies-Bergère, the legendary can-can club whose sexiness and spectacle have had a strong influence on mainstream fashion for a century now.

More than clothing, Baker wore strategically placed adornments: a faux banana here, a rhinestone there, leaving little to the imagination. Her severely short, slicked-down hair and her willingness to strip down to almost nothing expressed the new freedom that women were finally unafraid to strive for after the First World War. It's worth noting, though, that to be as sexually liberated as Baker, a woman living in the United States—rather than Paris—had to be famous, or white.

Most of us think of the late 1960s as the time when mainstream society began to acknowledge and accept the inevitability of sex before marriage, but the sexual revolution rumbled long before the Gloria Steinems of the world were but zygotes in their repressed mothers' wombs. Witness this excerpt of an essay by Samuel D. Schmalhausen, titled "Sex Among the Moderns" and published in the *Birth Control Review* (yes, such a periodical did exist) in October 1928:

Something strange and new and shatteringly real is happening in the world before our very eyes . . . the attempt of respectable women to win back . . . the sweet and disreputable bliss of spontaneous sex desire, squandered throughout the ages (and oh! so lavishly) upon courtesans, whores and prostitutes.

This fellow's bombastic prose, combined with his anachronistically amoral idealization of sex, puts him at the margins of society in the 1920s. But there's no question that at the time, the mainstream was finally beginning to acknowledge the pure pleasures offered by the physical body. After hundreds of years of molding and concealing women's bodies, designers began to reveal their customers' pure forms. And no one denied that this revelation was intended to *invite* as much as it was to titillate.

Louise Brooks, a dancer and silent film actress, had a jet-black Dutch-boy do and a gamine style. Her scandalously short skirts showed off the legs of a disciplined athlete, but she exhibited the flapper's signature rejection of authority with a foul mouth and an almost comical disdain for the Hollywood machine. In her memoir, *Lulu in Hollywood*, Brooks wrote that with a "straightforward confession of ignorance in dress," she embarked on shopping spree to a store called Milgrim's on New York City's Upper West Side in 1924. She was on the verge of stardom, and Milgrim's was the sort of place that produced authorized copies of European couture, adapting and tailoring every piece to suit each individual customer. This was the most popular way for well-heeled Americans to participate in global fashion. "When I came for my first fitting," Brooks wrote, "I met an exuberant Italian woman, who, because I had small, firm breasts, slashed my evening gowns almost to the navel. My back she left bare. Sitting at a nightclub or a restaurant table, I was a nearly naked sight to behold." >

After hundreds of years of concealing women's bodies, designers began to reveal their pure forms.

Undressed/Dressed Down

With its seamed bodice and fringed zigzag hem, this white dress was made for dancing—and a slight, boyish figure like the one belonging to Louise Brooks.

Far left Greta Garbo, still a brunette, in costume for her first American silent film, *The Torrent*, in 1926. Garbo played a small-town girl who became a smash on the world stage—and then, life imitated art.

Left Tamara de Lempicka's *Kizette in Pink*, which she painted in 1926. As a fiercely independent female artist, Lempicka first gained fame for a glamorous self-portrait in which she is driving a green Bugatti. Although the subject of this painting wears a tennis outfit, she's far from the court, illustrating the influence of Jean Patou's sportswear sensibility on society fashion.

< Just five years earlier, this sort of flesh display would have been considered tasteless and shunned by anyone but a prostitute. But as the flapper archetype was personified by dancing girls and silent film stars like Brooks, the body became the voice these women used to speak to the world. Brooks was reportedly fond of saying, "I like to drink and fuck," and this was evident in the way she dressed.

But Brooks, like all actresses working in the studio system, had little control of the way she appeared on screen. Hollywood studio heads were Svengalis, carefully constructing the personas of their contract actresses.

Where once melodramatic silent film stars had moped around in heavy nightgowns and dour expressions, now sprightly ingenues such as Clara Bow and Colleen Moore bopped about in fetishy boxing costumes, men's suits, and fringed minidresses—and sometimes, even, very little at all.

In France, meanwhile, the designer Jean Patou was at the forefront of a new trend for sportswear. First known for making functional athletic outfits—his daringly short tennis skirt for champion Suzanne Lenglen is an iconic example of his feminine take on activewear—Patou soon brought his mastery of knitwear and performance garments to the social arena, creating looks that showed off women's newly tanned and athletic physiques. Patou's iconoclastic, function-based take on high fashion extended beyond the realm of women's clothing: He also invented the men's designer neckwear category, using dressy silk fabrics to create natty, colorful ties.

A true lifestyle merchant, Patou not only pioneered the luxury fragrance business (his masterpiece, Joy, became perhaps the best known perfume of all time), but he also produced and marketed the first suntan oil, called Huile de Chaldée, in 1928.

Although he, of course, was French, Patou considered the ideal beauty to be American. Returning from a trip to the United States in 1924, Patou brought a harem of tall, lithe American models back with him to France to star in his fashion shows.

DESIGNER OF THE DECADE

Coco Chanel

Separating herself furthest from the pack was a young designer named Coco Chanel, who distilled the looser, shorter, freer silhouette of the twenties to its essence by executing it in unfussy materials and leaving it plain. Chanel rebelled against the traditional European conception of femininity. She kept an ultra-slim figure long before it was fashionable, and preferred being tan to having alabaster skin unspoiled by the sun. Instead of marrying, Chanel took lovers, and instead of homemaking—or starring in films, for that matter—she helmed a powerhouse of a company. This was an active, not a passive, woman.

Chanel started her career making hats, but unhappy with the lack of streamlined, unfussy clothing available to modern women, she soon transitioned to making dresses, and jackets as well. Rather than costly lace and silk, she employed inexpensive military fabric to make sheaths and—gasp!—trousers. Chanel incorporated traditional elements of menswear, such as pockets and lapels, into women's clothing. The silhouette she favored was often referred to as the "Garçonne" look, because it was more little-boy than grown-woman. To make her clothes appear as sporty and streamlined as possible, she bound chests to minimize breast projection and lowered waistbands to straighten the line of the

hips. The body-molding tactics Chanel employed were diametrically opposed to the goals of the recently ubiquitous corset, though there was something similar in the way each prescribed what a woman should look like. But while the lines of classic early Chanel had much in common with the flapper dresses that were shimmying across America at the same time, the overall gestalt of Chanel's aesthetic was one of athleticism rather than Dionysian frenzy.

Above Inspired by men's sportswear, the young Coco Chanel was reportedly fond of wearing her boyfriends' oversized cardigan sweaters—before she began designing her own.

Right The iconic Chanel look—layered knits, multiple strands of pearls, a mix of masculine (hat) and feminine (camellia) accessories—hasn't changed in almost one hundred years. Thank goodness.

The 1930s

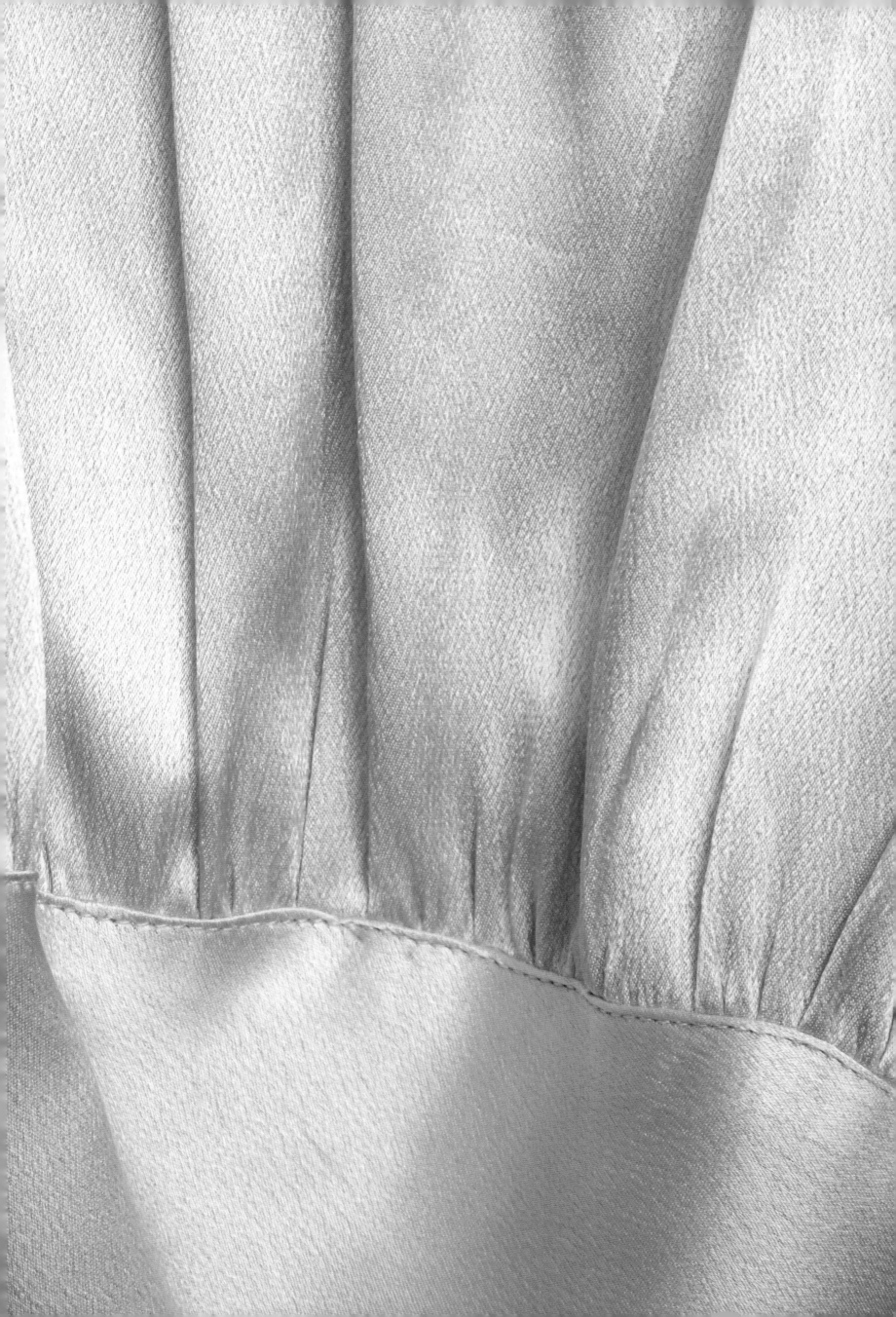

The look of the 1930s is what we still think of eighty years later as the ultimate expression of Hollywood glamour. In the golden age of Hollywood, "celebrity" designers—who dressed stars both on- and offscreen, and came from both the costume-design and high-fashion worlds—created an aesthetic of aspiration that pulled many spirits through the Great Depression and the beginning of the Second World War.

An important legacy of the thirties that we take for granted today, though, is the incorporation of ease and comfort into "serious" dressing. Whether it was putting a woman in a man's suit or using the bias, rather than a whalebone, to give a gown guts, the thirties made fashion unapologetically effortless. In the 1920s, all the rebels looked alike. But in the 1930s, getting dressed became a mode of self-expression.

If the 1920s were about playing with gender, then the '30s were about chasing it into a dark alley and beating it up. There was Amelia Earhart, with her boyish, athletic figure, short bob, and variety of chic jumpsuit and leather jacket combos that could saunter down any runway today, virtually unchanged. There was Eleanor Roosevelt, who, as the consoling, maternal presence leading America through the Great Depression, became an anti-fashion icon. The heiress Pancho Barnes escaped her

overbearing family by posing as a man and running off to Mexico. Even Wallis Simpson, who at first glance appears to epitomize restrained, ladylike femininity, was a sort of gender warrior, when you consider the power she had over the future king of England. But the ultimate gender warriors were the German actress Marlene Dietrich, who switched between tuxedos and evening gowns, and Frida Kahlo, whose provocative image balanced the yin and yang of male and female.

A number of cultural forces paved the way for this wildly rebellious expression of gender. Flapper culture allowed women to be less feminine and proper, more boyish and naughty. An abundance of factory jobs meant men were no longer the only ones to wear the pants. But perhaps the most powerful contributing factor was the cultural renaissance flourishing in Weimar Berlin between 1918 and 1933, in the years leading up to the Third Reich.

Most of us are familiar with this period of great intellectual thought and highly transgressive nightlife through the musical *Cabaret*, which was an adaptation of Christopher Isherwood's novel *Berlin Stories*. The show is chockablock with invigorating song-and-dance numbers, but a dark desperation permeates the entertainment—there's a sense you'll never really understand all that's going on beneath the surface of the lives of

these characters. Of course this darkness is a metaphor for fascism, Nazism, and intolerance in general—but it is also a testament to the tension and mystery of a time when all the social rules were changing.

The Weimar underground didn't represent the same brand of freewheeling anti-convention as flapper culture, even though the two overlapped time-wise. In Europe, the stakes were higher—the risks were real as fascism loomed. There was a darkness to this rebellion that simply wasn't as palpable in the U.S. version of the Roaring Twenties. It's almost as though the little boy who inspired the flapper look was forced to become a man.

Previous A delicate silk gown with a capelet and silk-satin belt from the thirties, by an anonymous designer.

Right Transatlantic pilot Amelia Earhart wears a leather pea coat, slim pants, and lace-up boots in 1930. "Adventure is worthwhile in itself," she once said. Her signature look came to represent the ultimate uniform for the modern independent woman—whether or not she had a pilot's license.

Far right Vionnet house model Sonia in 1937. She strikes a classical pose for photographer Horst P. Horst, wearing a sheer lamé gown fastened by a rhinestone closure at the neck.

Overleaf Margo Lion, who famously played Pirate Jenny in the original French version of Bertolt Brecht's *Threepenny Opera*—the ultimate expression of the Weimar cabaret sensibility—is also known for singing a scandalous duet with Marlene Dietrich, which glowed with lesbian overtones.

Marlene/Frida

The Weimar cabaret offered a distillation of all the social, political, and moral conventions that were about to explode in the 1930s. It showed great social and artistic innovation at the same time that hostility, dread, and danger were brewing just beneath the surface of virtually every human interaction. In cafe society, people of different cultures and classes intermingled, commiserated, and collaborated. Although people made time for celebration, they did so in the service of engaging with ideas and culture. No longer hedonism for hedonism's sake, the socializing in the time leading up to the Second World War was an era of bright-burning creative freedom.

The queen of the cabaret was Marlene Dietrich. Beautiful, singular, and Teutonic, she was a self-proclaimed "American" movie star as the United States geared up for a war against Germany. Most compelling about her was the fluidity of her sexuality and gender expression. When other women wore gowns, Dietrich wore tuxedos. When other women wore cloche hats, Dietrich wore fedoras. When other women spoke as though they'd been inhaling helium, Dietrich sounded as though she'd been gargling rocks. Dietrich must have known that she was regarded as an iconic sex object, but famously said, "I am, at heart, a gentleman."

As Peter B. Flint wrote in her *New York Times* obituary, in 1992, "The Dietrich image, personified by Lola-Lola, the seductive cabaret singer in top hat and silk stockings whom she portrayed in *The Blue Angel*, was that of a liberated woman of the world who chose her men, earned her own living and viewed sex as a challenge. Audiences were captivated by this creature out of no one's experience but out of everyone's imagination."

Like Dietrich, Frida Kahlo was keenly interested in the way she was perceived. In fact, she may have been the world's first performance artist. Decidedly feminine, Kahlo played with the visual signs of gender and was also openly bisexual. She famously exaggerated her facial hair, painting thick brown fuzz over her upper lip in all her self-portraits and highlighting her monobrow. Playing off these traditionally masculine signifiers were her outfits, based on the folkloric Tehuana costumes of indigenous Mexicans. >

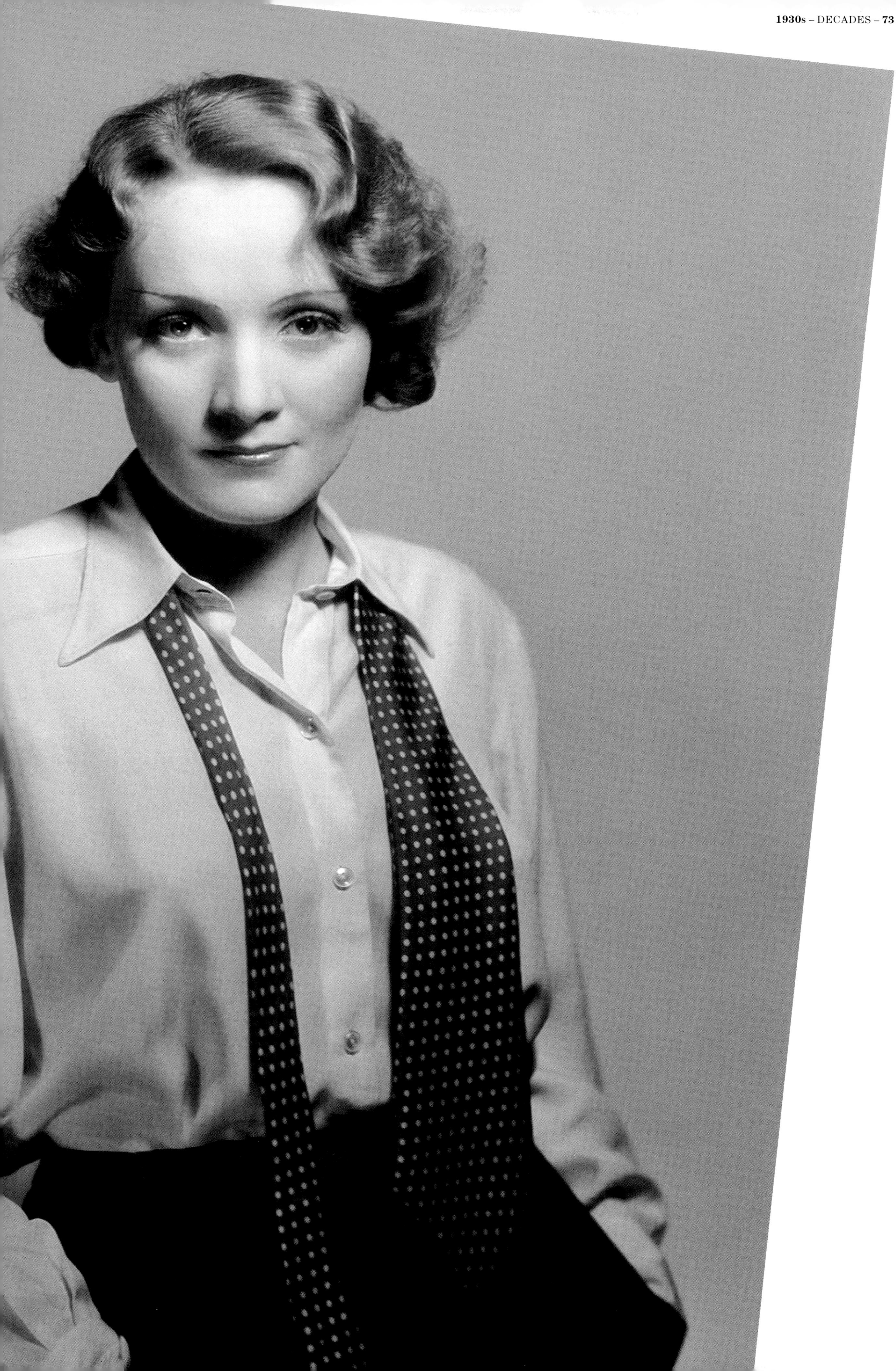

< Where we imagine Dietrich in black and white, Kahlo jumps out of history in Technicolor, whether because of the famous photographs taken of her by Nickolas Muray for *Vogue*, her paintings themselves, or the vividness of her persona.

Kahlo looked at clothing not only as a crucial tool in her artist's palette, but also as a document on which to preserve memories—a woven diary of sorts. After her death in 1954, her husband, Diego Rivera, stipulated that her bedroom and wardrobe be cordoned off for no less than fifty years before anyone could excavate. Just recently, among her beautiful skirts and dresses, researchers found a carefully preserved, blood-stained hospital gown that must have served as a painful reminder of the many surgeries she'd been forced to endure as a result of illness and accident.

Up until the 1930s, clothing had usually been employed by women in the service of simply "looking beautiful." Now, both Kahlo and Dietrich were imbuing it with much greater meaning. It wasn't only their gender play that connected Dietrich and Kahlo at the fashion vanguard of the early thirties, but also their almost postmodern knack for self-creation. Kahlo and Dietrich were each doing their own version of drag.

Kahlo both controlled people's perception of her in visual terms and manipulated a number of facts to support the myth that she created around herself throughout her life. Even though she was born in 1907, and so would have been three years old when the Mexican Revolution began, she claimed that she was born in 1910—the year it started—so people would associate her with it. She claimed that her father was of Jewish heritage—which would have held a certain subversive cachet in the years leading up to the Second World War—when his family was actually Lutheran and German.

Like Kahlo's, Dietrich's myth blurred the line between truth and fiction. Shortly after coming to Hollywood in 1930, she lost thirty pounds at the urging of director Josef von Sternberg, whom she was happy to acknowledge as her Svengali. She tweezed her eyebrows into thin, elegant arches, lightened her hair from brown to a suitably Teutonic blond, and even used clips along her hairline to manipulate the tautness of her face. Max Factor, the legendary makeup artist, covered her hair in real gold dust (which cost sixty dollars per ounce) so it would shine under the camera lights.

"Glamour," Dietrich said, "is assurance. It is a kind of knowing that you are all right in every way, mentally and physically and in appearance, and that, whatever the occasion or the situation, you are equal to it." Even though Dietrich and Kahlo couldn't have looked more different from each other, they shared a certain spirit of open rebelliousness and unbridled political activism, and they took total responsibility for themselves.

Kahlo looked at clothing not only as a tool in her artist's palette, but also as a woven diary of sorts.

Frida Kahlo on White Bench by photographer Nickolas Muray, taken in 1938. Kahlo and Muray reportedly carried on a passionate romantic relationship for more than a decade. Kahlo's floral headdress, medallion necklace, fringed shawl, and mixed botanical prints are traditional, but her look was totally modern.

Austrian actress and singer Dorit Kreysler in costume for the German film *Frischer Wind aus Kanada* (*A Fresh Wind from Canada*), in 1935.

Fantasy/Reality

Culturally, the 1930s were like a study in plate tectonics. The earth settled and shifted as it shouldered the aftershocks of the First World War, the stock market crash of 1929, and all the social-convention blasting that had taken place in the 1920s. Amid the devastation of the Great Depression and the terrifying heat that emanated from Weimar Berlin as it began its transition into the Third Reich, Hollywood's glamour fantasy promised a much-needed form of escape for people all over the world.

George Hurrell shot MGM's official publicity portraits of its megastars throughout the 1930s, and to this day, his photographs provide a master class in the study of elegant deception. In his portraits of everyone from Norma Shearer to Joan Crawford, he uses lighting to shape and perfect the faces of his subjects. It was Hurrell's belief that a woman's facial expression could afford her much more sexiness than her bare skin, and as he coached formerly white-bread starlets such as Shearer into bringing a come-hither look into their wide eyes, he brought their careers a new, dark dimension. "The most essential thing about my style was working with shadows to design the face instead of flooding it with light," he later said.

What Hurrell did to the faces of actresses, costume designers did to their bodies. The crown prince of costume design in the thirties was Gilbert Adrian, born Adrian Adolph Greenburg. Adrian started his career designing for the theater in New York, then fatefully accepted a contract with MGM Studios in 1928, and remained there until leaving to open his own studio in 1941. Adrian designed the most iconic film looks of the decade, from Greta Garbo's Anna Christie in 1930 to Judy Garland's Dorothy in *The Wizard of Oz* in 1939.

Adrian's talent for making stars look their best was unrivaled. His beadwork was subtly shaded to maximize the figure of the woman wearing it. He inventively employed the strategies of military tailoring—especially exaggerated shoulders—to create the strong, imposing look for which Joan Crawford became known. Perhaps even more important than his gift for trompe l'oeil was his ability to connect emotionally to the work of his famous clients. "You must never put costume jewelry or imitation lace on Garbo. Not that it would be noticed on the screen, but it would do something to Garbo and her performance," he said. That's what a truly great costume designer does. He helps an actress find her character.

Although in the 1940s Adrian was famous for doing Crawford's bold-shouldered day dresses and suits, it's his evening dresses that captivate us today. They look contemporary—they're truly timeless and impossible to pinpoint unless you're an expert. >

Hollywood's glamour fantasy promised a form of escape for people all over the world.

< A simple Adrian halter gown could be mistaken for a nineties Badgley Mischka or a seventies Halston. That's the beauty of great design, a quality that so eludes young designers these days. We have so much disposable fashion, so many fleeting moments. All the legacy designers who have long careers have really been able to create a distinctive DNA of what their style is and to establish true consistency of vision. As long as they build every idea off that foundation, they'll succeed. An aesthetic that's not based on trends doesn't go out of style.

In 1942, as the Second World War dimmed the Hollywood marquees, and film productions became less fantastical and more cost-conscious, Adrian shifted career directions, turning away from movie production and embracing the retail market full-tilt. He opened a boutique in Los Angeles and distributed thousands of "Gowns by Adrian" to stores in every single major city across the United States. A spectacular career dictating fashion for the masses—not just the matinee idols—stemmed out of his work in film. (In 1932, even before Adrian "officially" went into the fashion business, Macy's reported selling more than fifty thousand knockoffs of a gown he made for Joan Crawford in the film *Letty Lynton*.)

Adrian's contemporary at Paramount, where Marlene Dietrich was under contract, was Travis Banton. As Diana Vreeland

asserted in her book *Hollywood Costume*, Banton, unlike Adrian, was not so much obsessed by form and shape as he was by details that created character and drew attention to an actress's beauty. Vreeland explained,

Banton employed whole ranges of textures and surfaces from spangles to carnations. He amassed details—stockings with elaborate clocking, and so on. He echoed detail with detail, the lace of a mantilla caught in the lace of a parasol that was amplified by the lace through which the camera saw the scene.

Where Adrian's vision was subtle and filmic, Banton's was big and theatrical. The stars he dressed most frequently—Dietrich and Mae West—were the ideal expression of his theatrical point of view.

While Hollywood was the land of escape, Europe in the 1930s was bursting with propaganda, fear, and tension, in a desperate search for release. Many European artists and designers reacted by breaking from reality completely, venturing into an alternate universe of their own creation, which came to be known as Surrealism. The painter Salvador Dalí was the patriarch of the Surrealist clan, and avant-garde fashion designer Elsa Schiaparelli, or Schiap, as her inner circle referred to her, created a number of items that referenced his works. >

Right Four models wearing capes designed by Charles James, photographed in the mid-thirties. A true master of construction, James was known to work on a single sleeve for days on end.

Far right In 1933 Baron de Meyer captured this photograph of a dramatic Schiaparelli ensemble: a quilted cape worn over a shiny satin gown.

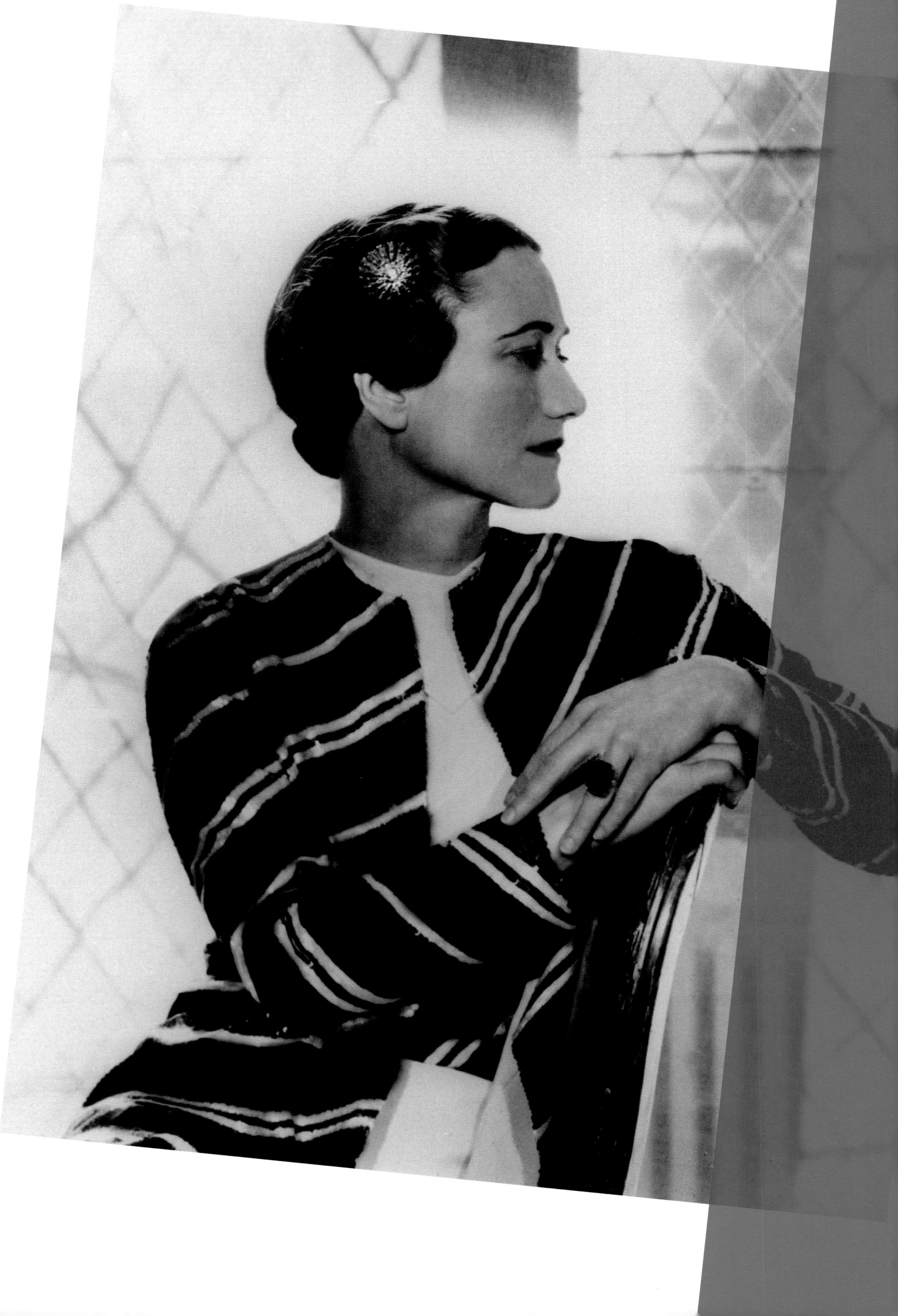

Far left Wallis Simpson in a
sequined candy-cane striped jacket,
paired with a jeweled hair accessory
and big black cocktail ring. It's no
wonder that Mrs. Simpson decided
to go by her middle name, Wallis
—she never really looked like
a "Bessie."

Left The Duke and Duchess
of Windsor the year after their
wedding in 1936, at Château de
Candé, France. The happy couple
met for the first time at a party
at the home of the then-prince's
then-mistress, Lady Thelma
Furness, in 1931.

Overleaf, left A model wears an
intricately pleated knit dress by
costume designer Joe Strassner,
in 1934. German by birth, Strassner
was responsible for creating
the costumes in many of Alfred
Hitchcock's most iconic films,
including *The 39 Steps* and
Sabotage.

Overleaf, right A shockingly
low-cut metallic evening gown
from 1930. This era produced some
of the most risqué looks of the
twentieth century.

< Her Lobster Dress of 1937 was a
collaboration with Dalí, who had been
using lobsters as a motif in his paintings
and sculptures for years. Although the
Lobster Dress is a fascinating link in a game
of cultural telephone, it's the kind of thing
that serves more as an artifact than an
element of a modern wardrobe.

Another Dalí–Schiap collaboration, the
Skeleton Dress, was made of black crepe
and used trapunto quilting to create a
sculptural understructure that mimicked
human bones, making it look as though the
wearer's skeleton was doing its best to creep
out from under her skin. Whether or not
Schiaparelli intended it to, the Skeleton
Dress invites an interesting discussion about
the role of a woman's body in fashion.

A frequent Schiaparelli client was Wallis
Simpson, later known as the Duchess of
Windsor. She was photographed by Cecil
Beaton in the Lobster Dress shortly before
she married Edward VII in 1937. Most
people know that Simpson was a socialite
who, despite being already twice divorced
and—perhaps even worse—American, so
besotted the king of England that he opted
to abdicate his throne rather than not marry
her. But many do not know that Simpson's
impeccably elegant image and projection
of ultimate self-control was a construction.
Though she portrayed herself as the ultimate
aristocrat, Simpson had actually spent
her childhood years in a state of relative
poverty. Although she always denied
having aggressively pursued the hand
of King Edward, every eyewitness to their
affair—including the close friend from
whom she reportedly stole her high-profile
beau—testified otherwise. But no matter
the opinions of others—Simpson ended
up one of the richest women in the world,
and a true fashion icon. (Even if you're
not a big fan of the duchess's politics or
personal protocol, she's so chic in that
cool, mean way.)

Mainbocher was Wallis Simpson's favorite designer. She chose him to design her wedding gown: a simple, elegant design that *Life* magazine called "the most copied dress in fashion history." Copies of "The Wally" were sold all over the United States, for prices that ranged from $8.90 to $250.

American-born, Mainbocher had an extensive career in fashion before becoming a designer. He started as a sketch artist for a clothing manufacturer, then moved into magazines, first at *Harper's*, then *Paris Vogue*, where he was promoted to chief editor. In 1929, he became the first American to open a couture house in Paris. His wasp-waisted sensibility was dramatically at odds with the looser constructions that had pervaded much of the 1920s and '30s, which is probably why it appealed to Simpson, who is credited with coining the infamous adage "One can never be too rich or too thin."

Mainbocher's designs oozed exclusivity, good breeding, and rarefied taste. Fashion editor Sally Kirkland is said to have remarked, "He made a woman look not only like a lady, but as if her mother had been a lady, too."

Mainbocher introduced the boned, strapless bodice in 1934, which, along with Madame Vionnet's slip (see page 38), has remained at the foundation of evening dresses ever since. His iconic corset, immortalized in 1939 by the famous photographer Horst P. Horst, is one of the sexiest fashion images ever made. But this sexuality is not about freedom —this image eroticizes the repression of a woman's body, not the emancipation of it. Mainbocher's clients, like his models, boasted slim, athletic forms, not the abundant flesh of women of the 1910s. His corset was purely for decoration, not function. Like Wallis Simpson, Mainbocher's designs derived their allure from control.

DESIGNER OF THE DECADE

Mainbocher

Mainbocher made a woman look not only like a lady, but as if her mother had been a lady, too.

A Mainbocher ensemble from 1936 features a dress, gloves, hat, and round belt buckle, all in the same fabric. "I have never known a really chic woman whose appearance was not, in large part, an outward reflection of her inner self," he once said. Presumably he imagined the thoughts of chic women to be awfully uniform.

The 1940s

When the United States officially entered the Second World War in 1941, life on the big screen needed to provide a better escape from real life than ever before. Because of rationing, new jobs, and a noticeable absence of men in everyday life, the gulf between the lives of real American women and the fictional characters they idolized was wider in the 1940s than in any other decade of the twentieth century.

As women projected their deepest desires onto the women of the big screen, Hollywood actresses became more adored than ever before. These stars almost seemed to belong to a separate caste of humanity, immune to war and quotidian concerns, and charged with a very important responsibility: keeping up the country's morale. The elevation of Hollywood stars into veritable deities meant that the time was right for the United States to become the style center of the world.

The Paris couture universe came to a halt when the Germans began their occupation in 1940. The Nazis shut down many fashion houses, leaving just twenty to continue operating as what were essentially exclusive ateliers for the wives of SS officers.

The United States was ready to pick up where Paris had left off. In America, where just a few years earlier no one had been able to find a job, there was now work for everyone—even women. Despite the undercurrent of sadness and fear over the war, there was also a new sense of possibility—that America would soon repossess the vigor that had defined it before the Great Depression. This complex optimism was evident in the way women were represented in advertising and war propaganda.

The original Rosie the Riveter was the star of a Norman Rockwell cartoon that graced the May 29, 1943, cover of the *Saturday Evening Post*. With her robust biceps, superior stare, and "patriotic" coloring—red hair, white skin, blue coveralls—Rosie is depicted as crushing Hitler's life's work effortlessly with one strong foot.

This image of woman was opposite that of the sylphlike flapper girls and sinewy, sparkle-gowned starlets who had been ruling magazine covers for the past twenty years. The Second World War was the first war in which women played a pivotal role, contributing to the war effort instead of just abstractly supporting the men behind it. >

Previous Detail of a ruby-red satin gown with buttons, designed by Jacques Fath in the forties. The intricate, multilayered neckline reflects Fath's mastery of the almost origami-like construction technique that he pioneered.

Right Two women at work assembling a Vega aircraft during the Second World War. Although the war was the impetus that brought women into the workplace in the forties, they stayed there even after peace was declared.

Far right Actress Elizabeth Taylor in 1945. Unlike many starlets who called upon Hollywood costume designers and studio vaults to put together their red-carpet looks, Taylor chose and purchased all her clothing herself, directly from couturiers.

< Despite all the tragedy of the forties, visual references of the time show a deep-seated belief in romantic love and an optimism that no one had seen in a while—almost a romantic moralism. America became the bastion of the Good.

Patriotic images of women came in two flavors: strong and sexy. Women dressed up as soldiers, or undressed as pinups. In this new economy, some women manufactured the products while other women *were* the products. Pinups were an American export—literally—torn from magazines and taken on tour with GIs all over the world, to be "pinned up" in their lockers as a sort of early virtual girlfriend or blow-up doll.

Artist Alberto Vargas created the iconic illustrated pinups, serialized in *Esquire* magazine, which came to be known as Varga Girls. From their first appearance in December 1940, they were an international sensation. Pinup culture was about an idealization of beauty, a fetishization of type. It was not about the clothes, for these gals didn't wear much. These simple images of exaggerated sexuality were almost like cartoons—copies of copies that brought comfort in their familiarity, as well as a cheap thrill.

It was only a matter of time before the pinup girls were being used not only to assuage the loneliness of GIs abroad but also to sell products to their wives, stateside. As the men left their daily lives for war, women took society's center stage in the forties. A new feminine power was evident in the trends that swept the United States and Europe, including the triangle silhouette (big shoulders, narrow hips), high-waisted pants, red lipstick, and platform shoes.

The one thing you didn't see any "regular" gals wearing? Gowns. But you could still find these expensive, theatrical confections on Hollywood film stars. Like their gowns, these screen icons were the only sort of women in the forties who could afford not to be mass-produced.

Patriotic images of women came in two flavors: strong and sexy.

Previous, left Actress Yvonne De Carlo in 1948. Although she appears quite wholesome in this photo, De Carlo actually found fame portraying a host of risqué characters, from Salome to "Slave Girl" to femme fatale.

Previous, right A famous wartime pinup known as "The Polka-Dot Girl," Chili Williams models a leopard-skin bathing suit, originally designed by Ed Hamilton for winter beach resorts.

Left A vision of sophistication in August 1941, this model wears the sort of dress, hat, and gloves that exemplified the new working woman's daytime uniform.

Joan/Rita

Although Hollywood costumes in the 1940s weren't as lavish as they had been in the previous decade, the actresses who wore them were more glamorous than ever before. They were no longer charged with *inspiring* the style of real women, but with *replacing* it.

There were two kinds of Hollywood actress. The Consumer, represented by ball-busting broad Joan Crawford, was a new kind of woman in charge of her own destiny, a true individual. The Consumed, epitomized by the glossy-haired, soft-eyed Rita Hayworth, was a projection of the American male fantasy, ripe for the picking.

Arguably the most popular actress of her time, Crawford didn't tart around in evening dresses dripping with diamonds; rather, she appeared, without fail, as a preternaturally poised, strong woman. Her signature triangle silhouette, invented by costume designer Gilbert Adrian (see page 76), boasted broad, powerful shoulders that balanced out her womanly hips. Although Crawford was only five feet four inches, she appeared much taller. At a time when women were serving a crucial function out in the world—not only at home—Crawford represented a self-sufficient icon who empowered, inspired, and made no apologies. Both on-screen and off, her look reflected this. One might say Crawford was the first feminist movie star.

Rita Hayworth took the image of a Varga Girl and brought it to life. An iconic redhead,

she was actually born a raven-haired Latina. In order to become an "American" movie star, she underwent a massive transformation—an element of which was, famously, the raising of her hairline—in order to look the way she did at the height of her fame.

One of Hayworth's defining roles was Rusty in 1944's *Cover Girl*, a sweet and anonymous dancer who gets plucked out of a Brooklyn chorus line by a publishing mogul and becomes a modeling sensation—sort of a proto–*Pretty Woman*. The message in *Cover Girl* reflects a different society from the one in *Pretty Woman*, though: Rusty gets everything she thinks she wants, but the indulgent lifestyle of the model/starlet fails to bring her happiness. The implication is that she'd be happier back in Brooklyn, living poor and honest with her true love. This is, of course, where she ends up. Playing characters like Rusty, Hayworth seemed more like the women devouring her movies than the woman starring in them.

The dichotomy illustrated by Crawford and Hayworth is an early example of the eternal dilemma in Hollywood today: achieving the delicate balance between aspirational and accessible. Hollywood costume designers continued to exert a strong influence on trends in both high and low fashion because the only women who could afford—financially or morally—to dress to the nines were movie stars.

Above Joan Crawford with Gilbert Adrian, the legendary costumer who dressed her in twenty-eight films (and for innumerable personal appearances). Adrian is credited with creating Crawford's signature powerful on-screen look, which usually included bold shoulders, nipped-in waists, and strong lapels that drew attention to her iconic face.

Right Part of Crawford's allure was her ability to look domineering and intimidating one moment, exquisitely feminine the next. By the height of her career, she represented the ultimate in the new ideal of postwar beauty.

Left Actress Rita Hayworth in costume for the 1946 film *Gilda*. For men all over the world, her role as the title character became synonymous with seduction. As she famously put it, "Every man I knew went to bed with Gilda . . . and woke up with me."

Above Making the white halter dress iconic even before Marilyn Monroe wore it decades later, in the sixties, Hayworth elevated the cheesecake photo to a new level of elegance and ideal beauty.

Left An iconic, drapey design by Madame Grès, so timeless it could be from classical Greece or today. The cultivation of this elemental quality was intentional. "For a dress to survive from one era to the next, it must be marked with an extreme purity," Grès once said.

Overleaf, left A model dances nude in a red scarf by Claire McCardell in 1946. McCardell's designs were bare not only because she aimed to create clothes that made women feel free, but also because fabric was at a premium during the Second World War.

Overleaf, right A design by Claire McCardell, photographed by Genevieve Naylor in Bermuda, in 1946. Rather than try to restructure the female form, McCardell's designs celebrated its natural shape. "Clothes may make the woman, but the woman can also make the clothes. When a dress runs away with the woman, it's a horror," she told *Time* magazine.

Foreigners/American Girls

Madame Grès saw life as her very own reinvention tour. Alix Grès, a.k.a. Alix Barton, a.k.a. Alix, a.k.a. Germaine Krebs, launched her Paris couture house, called Grès, in 1942, only to be forced to close it six months later because of the war. She was visibly defiant during the war years, refusing to obey the rules of fabric rationing and declining an offer to dress the wives of Nazi soldiers.

A classically trained sculptor who married a painter, Grès approached couture as a fine art. But instead of restricting and remolding the body, she sought to immortalize it, by wrapping it up in fabric. Grès shared her obsession with classical statuary with her spiritual godmother, Madame Vionnet (see page 38), and like Vionnet, she draped many of her gowns out of one massive bolt of material. Where Madame Grès truly struck out on her own, though, was in incorporating large bare areas into her designs. Although the display of skin must have seemed racy at the time, Grès was taking inspiration directly from bare-midriffed statues such as the Nike of Samothrace, which she had likely seen on display at the Louvre Museum.

In contrast to the mysterious and foreign approach of Madame Grès, the approach that designer Claire McCardell—who was as American as apple pie—took in dressing the women of the 1940s was unapologetically pragmatic. In doing so, she invented not only her own label but also a new category of fashion that has ruled ever since: American sportswear.

What inspired McCardell were the clothes she wanted to wear herself, in the real world—not to the opera, but to the office. McCardell embraced the newly democratic culture brought on by the war, and aimed to have the most exclusive label in fashion as well as the most inclusive. "I belong to a mass-production country where any of us, all of us, deserve the right to good fashion and where fashion must be available to all," she proclaimed.

Lest you believe McCardell lacked the technical expertise of her couture counterparts, know this: She could take a couture garment apart and put it back together again. As a young woman living at the Three Arts Club on West Eighty-fifth Street in Manhattan, she had access to the abandoned high fashion of wealthy philanthropists who supported young artists. This was her method of self-education and her signature aesthetic: deconstructing a garment and then reconstructing it in the smartest and most elegant manner possible. "I worked in the couture tradition—expensive fabrics, hand stitching, exclusivity, all that—but Claire could take five dollars' worth of common calico and turn out a dress a smart woman could wear anywhere," remarked one of her contemporaries, the designer Norman Norell. >

< Norell had such faith in McCardell's originality and talent that when he won the first Coty fashion award, in 1943, he said that McCardell should have won it instead.

McCardell's ethos had a lot in common with Coco Chanel's, in that both believed the job of clothing was to equip a woman to live her best life. "I like comfort in the rain, in the sun, for active sports, comfort for sitting still and looking pretty," McCardell said. Women voted with their pocketbooks in agreement with her philosophy. As Sally Kirkland noted in her book *All-American: A Sportswear Tradition*, McCardell sold thousands of the first wrap dress at a price of just $6.95 each.

Before striking out on her own in 1940, McCardell worked at the atelier of Hattie Carnegie. Carnegie was born Henrietta Kanengeiser, a Jewish girl in Vienna, but to ensure the success of her business she renamed herself after the wealthiest man in the world, Andrew Carnegie. One in the long line of wildly successful designers who started out making hats—what is it about hats?—Carnegie owned and ran a miniature department store off Manhattan's tony Fifth Avenue, where, in addition to her own designs, she sold imported French couture. She reportedly traveled to Paris as many as seven times a year to ensure that her customers stayed up to date with couture trends. By selling her label wholesale to department stores across the country, and devoting an area in her store to selling lower-priced, more casual sportswear to her younger customers, Carnegie pioneered many of the strategies that keep the fashion business running today. And McCardell was not the only legendary American designer to start her career at Hattie Carnegie: Also in her company were style giants James Galanos, Norman Norell, and Travis Banton.

Carnegie was more of a lifestyler than a dressmaker—her elegant, wholly American vibe appealed to high-profile women such as Joan Crawford, who wanted their persona to be one of intelligent glamour. "If you have a dress that is too often admired, be suspicious of it," Carnegie said, exhibiting her philosophy that the function of a wardrobe is to illuminate its wearer, not call attention to itself.

Left In the 1940s, it was not unusual for women to sew their own outfits—even getups as complicated as this one. This dress, in robin's egg blue, is accented with bows atop each shoulder and gold accessories.

Right A model wears a light blue moiré hood with red detailing, designed by Hattie Carnegie, from 1943. Nowadays, sporting a hood such as this one would be considered a fashion risk, but fifty years ago, it was the perfect uniform for dropping the kids at school. Those were the days . . .

As New York became the hotbed of the new American sportswear, Paris couture culture was in danger of being rendered obsolete. Dampened by an oppressive German regime, France's aesthetic primacy—as well as its export economy—was in danger.

Representatives of the fabric industry approached famed designer Christian Dior in desperation, hoping he'd deliver a new trend that would get their mills spinning nonstop once more.

Dior delivered, in the form of his New Look, in 1947. He strove to erase the pain of wartime by presenting a collection that departed from current trends in every way possible—and one that, of course, demanded lots and lots of expensive French fabric. "We were leaving a period of war, of uniforms, of soldier-women with shoulders like boxers," he explained. "I turned them into flowers, with soft shoulders, blooming bosoms, waists slim as vine stems, and skirts opening up like blossoms." This new, romantic vision set the tone for most of the next decade.

Right Designer Charles James fits a gown for Austine Hearst, wife of the famous newspaper and magazine publisher William Randolph Hearst Jr. This dress was just one of many commissioned by Hearst, perhaps James's most loyal patron.

Far right A model wears a coat made of skunk fur by Christian Dior, and clutches a red calfskin handbag with one hand, a mirror in the other.

New York/New Look

Although she lived in New York, the only designer more Hollywood than Gilbert Adrian (see page 76) was known as Valentina. A former drama student, Valentina took inspiration from the bias-cut works of Madame Vionnet (see page 38)—but unlike the dowdy Vionnet, she wore the clothing she designed.

Valentina used her mysterious feminine aura to convince beautiful women that she knew them better than they knew themselves. Not only did her clothes transform a woman's image, but they could also transform her career. Quietly advising megastars such as Greta Garbo on how to create the most alluring persona, she was a female Pygmalion. "My shop is like a clinic where I treat patients for bad taste," she was fond of saying.

Valentina's aesthetic was the opposite of obvious; where many would think to expose a star's assets, she concealed them instead. Her clothes were monastic, inspired by the humble, devotional robes of nuns. Not interested in cheap thrills, she strove to invent garments that transformed from one must-have into another, solving everyday wardrobe problems while still providing glamour and excitement through unexpected color combinations and lush materials, which gave her creations an idiosyncratic, at times even eccentric vibe.

The first image Valentina overhauled was her own. Born in Russia, she fled to Europe at the start of the revolution and then eventually came to the United States in 1923. In New York, she quickly went from struggling as an out-of-work actress to living the life of a style guru, swiftly acquiring a roster of clients any established couturier would envy. Valentina spoke as though she were reading from a self-help book co-authored by Ayn Rand and Diana Vreeland, insisting, "No matter how broke you are, always travel first class—otherwise you'll never meet the right kind of people."

She lived in the same building as Greta Garbo, whom she made her very close friend and devotee—and whom some claim that her husband, George Schlee, made his mistress. "What you wear in your own home is like a costume for the role of yourself," Valentina reportedly said. She also administered her glamour to Katharine Hepburn, Gloria Swanson, and Rosalind Russell. Harold Koda has written that Valentina's "career as an actress perhaps contributed to her ability to imbue her clothes with the multiple narratives of status, occasion and fantasy so seductive to her clients. And useful to the construction of her own compelling image." According to the *New York Times*, she started off with a bang: Her first year's sales, in a store she established with just thirteen dresses from her own wardrobe, totaled more than ninety thousand dollars.

DESIGNER OF THE DECADE

Valentina

Valentina sits for Horst P. Horst in the bedroom of her New York apartment in 1948, dressed in a mauve-and-red traditional sari. Valentina once called herself "the Gothic version" of Greta Garbo, but this image clearly represents her global-glam phase.

Not only did Valentina's clothes transform a woman's image, but they could also transform her career.

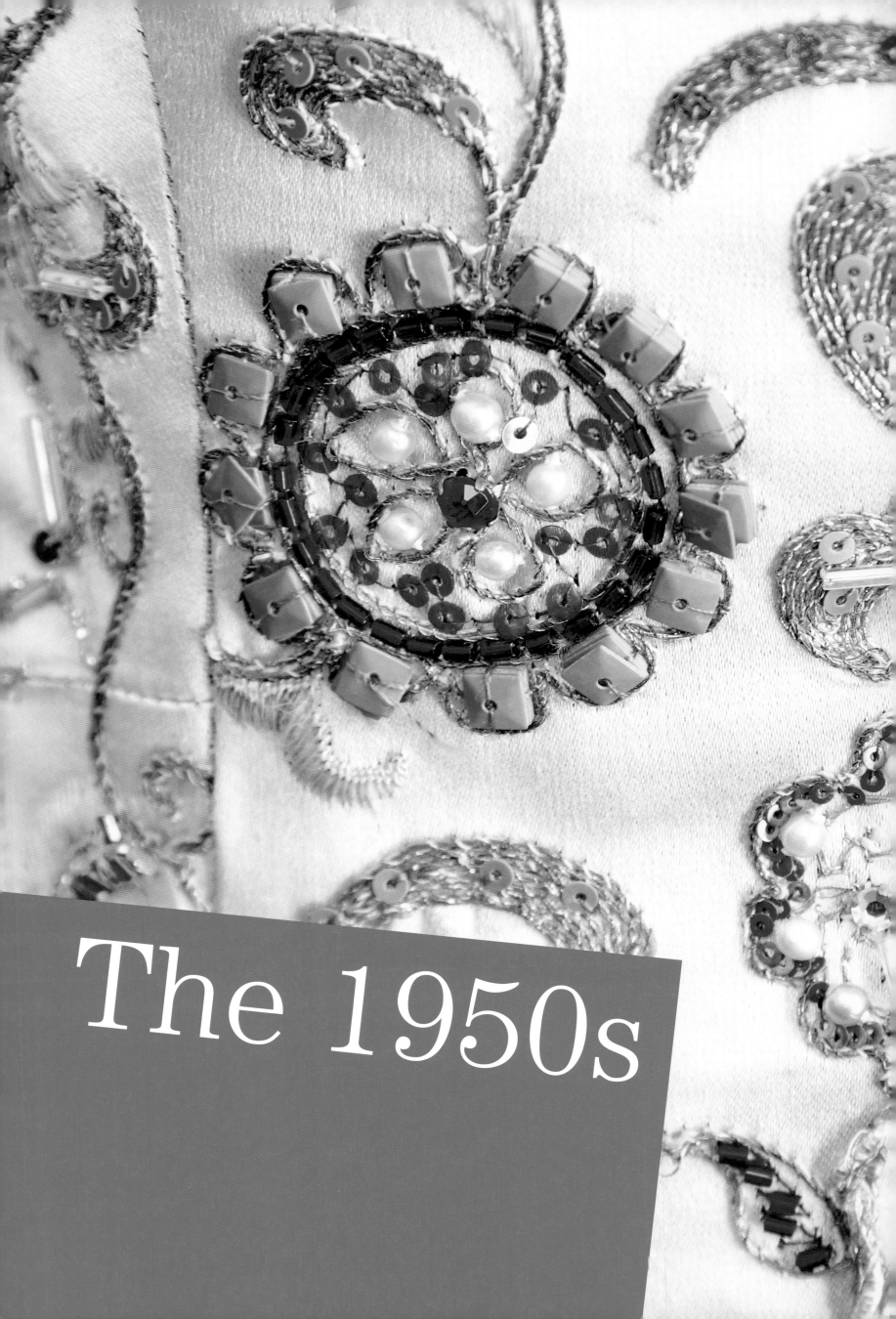

The 1950s

Color television was invented in the fifties, but it was still a decade lived almost entirely in black-and-white. TV shows and movies featuring the "typical" (read: flawless) American family served as road maps for real-world happiness. Social and cultural rules were clear. Gender roles reverted to the formality they'd occupied before the turn of the century. Even though this middle decade is known for its full-skirted, whitewashed, picket-fenced splendor, the dark side of the fifties was just as influential, if not more so. And it certainly made for interesting fashion.

Amid all the Doris Day musicals and Jell-O molds, American counterculture was coming to the forefront. Beatniks forsook bouffants for berets, migrated west, and practiced a doped-up, disobedient civility. A select group of veteran forties pinups—Bettie Page being the most "notorious"—traded their negligees and submissive gazes for corsets and whips, in open acknowledgment of long-hidden sexual subcultures. The reckless masculine ideal represented by James Dean and Jackson Pollock ran its motorcycle over the stereotype of the noble family man and war hero that had ruled the country through most of the previous decade. And tormenting every *Leave It to Beaver* family was a metaphorical Eddie Haskell, a simmering, contrarian force slowly plotting a secret scheme of rebellion, preparing to take over the world. It may have taken until the 1960s for all hell to break loose, but the 1950s were the time for laying the groundwork.

However encouraging the fifties were to the dark side, those years were also known, of course, as the "Golden Age of Couture." After the Second World War came to a close, the Paris couture houses, which had been shuttered by the Germans, reopened for business. Christian Dior's New Look in 1947 made Paris once again the place to go if you needed to get capital-D Dressed. Wealthy women from all over the world reopened their couture accounts. The United States had been deprived of its French fix since the onset of the war, and while this led to the development of a singular brand of American sportswear—the wardrobe equivalent of a quick and snappy Automat burger—the fashion class was ready for some haute cuisine again.

Previous Detail of a Christian Dior strapless gown called Palmyre, from around 1952. Versions of this spectacular jeweled gown were owned by both Marlene Dietrich and Mrs. Charles Chaplin.

Right In 1958, an impeccably dressed woman commands attention of passersby and paparazzi at the Paris couture shows.

After the Second World War came to a close,
the Paris couture houses reopened for business.

Left This 1957 photograph by
Loomis Dean originally appeared
in *Life* magazine. Taken in Paris,
it features models wearing a range
of designs by Christian Dior.

Overleaf, left Just evocative
enough, but not too racy for a
genteel dinner party, the bare-backed
dress became a favorite feature in
the closets of those on a quest to
get away with something.

Overleaf, right Photographed
by Horst P. Horst, this silk organdy
dress from the mid-fifties is accented
with a tangle of twisted beaded
necklaces. The model poses daintily
to accentuate her slender waist, but
the expression on her face tells its
own story. There's a smouldering
sensuality simmering beneath that
hot pink fabric.

Grace Kelly in costume on the set of Alfred Hitchcock's *To Catch a Thief* in 1955—just a year before she became princess of Monaco. This white silk-chiffon gown was created by legendary costume designer Edith Head. "I've dressed thousands of actors, actresses and animals," Head once remarked, "but whenever I am asked which star is my personal favorite, I answer, 'Grace Kelly.'"

Grace/Bettie

Blond and beatific, soft-spoken and flawless, Grace Kelly was idealized American Beauty incarnate. Her wasp waist and perfectly coiffed hair were symbols of restraint, and the yards and yards of fabric it took to make one just one of her size-four skirts served as a satin beacon of victory, prosperity, and hope.

Kelly's screen presence in *Rear Window* is an eloquent metaphor for a cultural perspective on fashion in the fifties. This beautiful but somewhat untouchable woman is taking up all the space in her boyfriend's apartment—with her skirt. The endless yardage of fabric seems to offer a cloud of expensive protection around a national treasure.

Had Bettie Page appeared in *Rear Window*, she would have been on the other side of the glass, outside in the street, commanding Jimmy Stewart's attention—and probably Grace Kelly's, too. The mirror image of Kelly in every possible way—brunette not blond, voluptuous not sylphlike, dominant not submissive—Page and her overt sexuality paved the way for virtually every modern performer/sexpot today, from Madonna to Lady Gaga.

Whips, chains, leopard-print, girl-on-girl action—no taboo was off-limits for a Page pictorial. Bettie Page would have looked less naked if she had worn nothing at all, rather than the leopard and leather bondage bikinis she frequently donned. Her exaggerated black bangs and red lipstick simultaneously beckoned men and pushed them away. She was a tease in every sense. Often the most powerful element of Page's pictures is her complicated gaze. On one hand, she appears challenging. On the other, she's supremely vulnerable in acknowledging her existence as the physical manifestation of someone else's sexual desire. All women in the 1950s were playing a role of some kind—Bettie Page just wasn't afraid to show the world that she knew it.

Below Bettie Page—the platonic form of pinups—poses suggestively in an open-sided leopard maillot, alongside a leopard almost as fierce as she is, in 1954.

Right Despite the fact that Bettie Page is, unquestionably, a style icon, she saw herself as existing outside the realm of trends. "I never kept up with the fashions," she said. "I believed in wearing what I thought looked good on me."

Bettie Page would have looked less naked if she had worn nothing at all.

In 1953, Coco Chanel reopened her house to great anticipation after shutting it down in 1939. Although her business had shuttered because of the war, many say that Chanel resurrected her label because she couldn't stand to see the fussy fashions of Monsieur Dior dominating the couture scene. "Dressing women is not a man's job," she said at the time. "They dress them because they scorn them."

Chanel's fashion philosophy was one of self-sufficiency: the Chanel customer should never need to ask a husband (or lover) to zip up the back of her punishing dress. Easy shapes formed from soft jersey and luxe wools gave a woman freedom. A simple palette and bold accessories gave her confidence. The comeback collection that she presented on February 5, 1954, was vintage Chanel—anchored by her iconic suits and simple white blouses.

While the collection failed to find immediate critical success—critics were reportedly underwhelmed, feeling Chanel had delivered looks they'd seen twenty-five years before—women clamored to buy it straight out of the gate. In a postwar era when the world was desperate to get "back to normal," pushing women into the kitchen and men out into the workplace, Chanel refused to turn back the clock. Even at seventy years old, she remained the coolest of the cool girls. >

Designers/Designed

Taken during what I lovingly refer to as Coco Chanel's "comeback tour," this photograph from the fifties illustrates the timelessness of Chanel's signature look—pearls, brooch, black jacket—more than thirty years after it was originally conceived.

The comeback collection was vintage Chanel—anchored by her iconic suits.

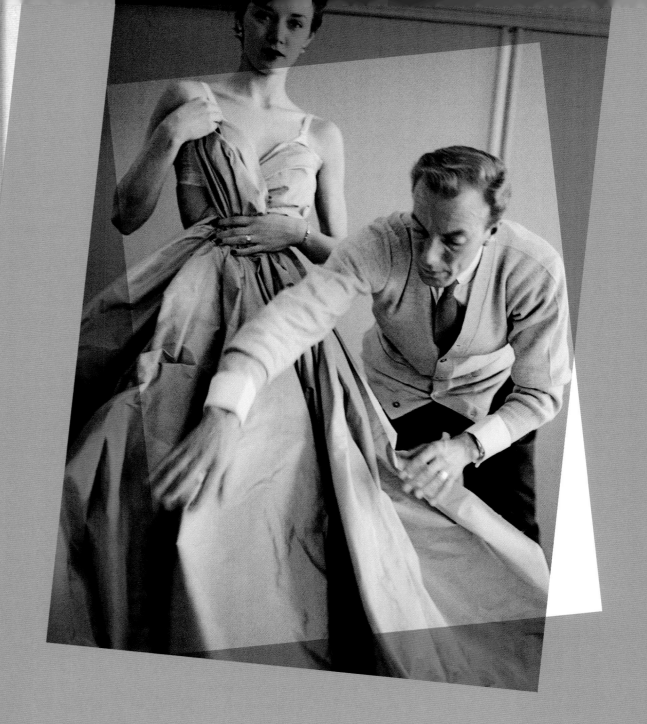

Left Claire McCardell's designs combined femininity and functionality for a vibe at once vulnerable and strong. Combining the sporty styling of a button-down shirt with the grandness of a ball skirt was trailblazing, but also somehow classic.

Above Jacques Fath drapes a ball gown on his fit model in 1951. Some of the most important designers of the twentieth century trained under this Parisian designer—Hubert de Givenchy, Guy Laroche, and Valentino Garavani among them.

< Chanel may have been the only European woman concerned with making clothes for a stylish everyday life, but this discipline had been flourishing in the United States ever since the Second World War had cut America off from its couture habit. Claire McCardell continued the innovative work she'd done in the forties. "I've always designed things I needed myself," she said, in an attempt to explain the wild popularity of her utilitarian but also playful collection. "It just turns out that other people need them, too."

Another young New York designer, named Bonnie Cashin, also made what she wanted to hang in her own closet, inventing what we now think of as layered dressing. After a stint in Hollywood in the forties, she returned east to design ready-to-wear, and immediately received both the Neiman Marcus and the Coty fashion awards, in 1950. Cashin put rich details on pieces she intended to be worn by women whom she called "modern nomads" through the varied activities of their lives. She mixed leather, fur, and hardware into her everyday designs, giving them a utilitarian chic that would greatly influence designers such as Marc Jacobs.

Anne Klein was the first major designer to focus on what the market then called "junior sophisticates." She developed and honed her aesthetic for this young and active customer, so when her business expanded to include older women in the 1960s, it always retained the blush and movement of youth.

While a new crop of innovative women designers followed in Chanel's footsteps, creating the essentials they longed to see hanging in their own closets, an old guard of male designers continued the timeless tradition of dressing women to look like delicious cupcakes, beckoning for men's consumption.

Chief among these confectioners was Jacques Fath, who molded stiff, luxurious fabrics into gowns that minimized the waist, emphasized the bust, and glorified the hips and bottom. Another champion of *la bella figura* was Roman designer Emilio Schuberth, who used strapless silhouettes, ultra-feminine fabrics, and fancy lace overlays to create a sultry, quintessentially Italian look.

Below This ensemble is from 1953, but it could just as well have come fresh off the catwalk today. The gold vest layered over a white button-down and tucked into aqua shorts creates an ultra-modern look.

Right Claire McCardell's red sundress from 1957 embodies the freedom and self-confidence she was known for. Although the halter-top construction and cinched waist seem effortless, they actually demonstrate a high level of technical mastery.

A new crop of designers followed in Chanel's footsteps, creating essentials they longed to see in their own closets.

Balenciaga remained a Spaniard at heart, always managing to infuse the essence of Spain into his creations.

The most innovative male couturiers of the 1950s were more architects than fashion designers, testing the limits of fabric and sewing to create works of suspension and aerodynamics as beautiful and complicated as the world's most breathtaking buildings. Demonstrating a masterful control of drape and proportion were Pierre Balmain, Charles James, and Hubert de Givenchy, but the most brilliant and accomplished of these visionaries was the Spanish couturier Cristóbal Balenciaga.

The son of a seamstress who began his own career designing bespoke gowns for the local aristocracy and eventually became dressmaker of choice to the Spanish royal family, Balenciaga left his home country in 1937, when the civil war forced him to shutter his ateliers in San Sebastián, Madrid, and Barcelona.

Immediately upon his arrival in Paris, Balenciaga proved himself to be a true couturier in the classical French sense, but he remained a Spaniard at heart, always managing to infuse the essence of Spain into his creations. Baby-doll dresses featured tiers of lace reminiscent of mantillas; column gowns were punctuated with dramatic silk cummerbunds that evoked triumphant matadors. The designer repeatedly drew inspiration from the work of Spanish artists such as Velázquez,

Goya, and El Greco, bringing the drama of the canvas into the everyday lives of the women who wore his designs.

During the decade when most of his peers were shrinking waistlines and inflating skirts, Balenciaga was inverting these proportions. In doing a series of radical design experiments throughout the fifties, he established the cuts and shapes of the fashions of the future. In 1950, at the height of popularity of Dior's wasp-waisted New Look, Balenciaga diverted attention away from the midriff, adding breadth to women's shoulders and volume to their backs. In 1953, when the masses were adorning their necks in pearls, Balenciaga devotees were resting their heads on the stiff collars of their balloon jackets. The designer also went against the grain inventing the baby-doll dress, the sack dress, the cocoon coat, and the chemise.

Unlike more traditional styles, whose shapes relied on corsetry, Balenciaga's designs used the body as their architecture and employed fabric to express the beauty of pure form. He used heavy textiles, substantial enough to hold the innovative, structural forms he created away from the body. Paradoxically, although Balenciaga's pieces camouflaged the female shape, they also did a masterful job of highlighting it.

DESIGNER OF THE DECADE

Balenciaga

Balenciaga combined the hallmarks of French couture with signifiers of his Spanish heritage. This ensemble from 1953 features a portrait neckline and delicate waist straight out of the Ritz Paris with a brocade fabric and jaunty black hat stolen from the bullring—or flamenco den.

The 1960s

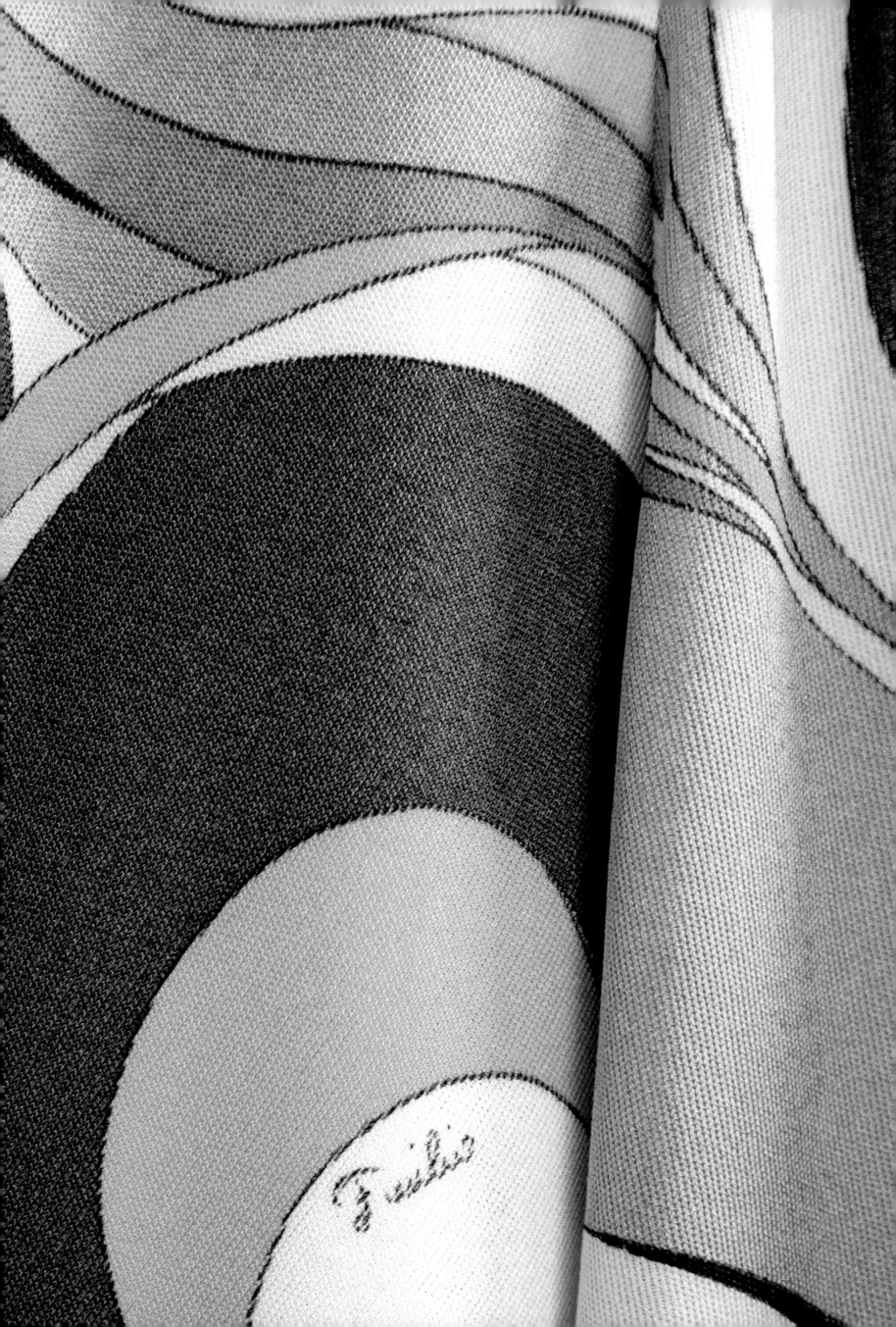

Many people think *The Graduate*, Mike Nichols's iconic masterpiece of suburban malaise, is about Dustin Hoffman's character's struggle to break free from the stifling, conventional world of his parents. It is. But it's also an epic battle between Anne Bancroft and Katharine Ross—between leopard print and corduroy, black and white, woman and girl. Between the past and the future. The film reveals a fundamental shift in the perception of beauty that took place in the 1960s: The feminine ideal was no longer the sexy mother, but her teenage daughter.

In *The Graduate*, Hoffman plays Benjamin Braddock, fresh out of college, spending some time at home in order to decide how to spend the rest of his life. He soon finds himself alone with the wife of his father's business partner, a bored and dangerous housewife played by Bancroft, who is dead-set on deflowering him. "Mrs. Robinson, you're trying to seduce me . . . aren't you?" Hoffman says, more terrified than coy.

"Would you like me to seduce you?" she responds, in a commanding tone that first became familiar to many people today when it was sampled in a George Michael song.

The first time we see her, Bancroft wears a gunmetal metallic shift that seems poured onto her waspy frame like quicksilver frozen in time. Over this armor floats a diaphanous layer of black silk chiffon, which makes Bancroft seem like a Sicilian widow traveling through outer space, an Italian cinema heroine transposed into John F. Kennedy's America. When Mrs. Robinson disrobes, much to Benjamin's horror and fascination, we see she is wearing a leopard-print lingerie ensemble. Later in the film, she appears in a twenty-five-thousand-dollar Somalian leopard-skin wrap. One wonders whether some of the recent affinity for comparing older women to exotic cats found its genesis in Mrs. Robinson's wardrobe. With her skins and streaks, pencil skirts and lace, Mrs. Robinson might as well have been dressed by Dolce and Gabbana.

Benjamin and Mrs. Robinson enjoy a tawdry affair, achieving an angst-ridden harmony in their relationship—until he meets her daughter.

Elaine Robinson is everything her mother is not. Instead of a well-coiffed pageboy bouffant, she has lank, middle-parted locks. Her eyes are bright and doelike, not sad and calculating. When Benjamin takes her out for the first time, against the stern warning of her jealous mother, she wears a snow-white double-breasted coat that cloaks her in an aura of purity and potential. >

Previous Detail of a jumpsuit created by Emilio Pucci in the 1960s. Pucci's proto-psychedelic silk confections defined what we now think of as "resort"—easy, luxurious ready-to-wear designed to complement the beauty and lifestyle of the transcontinental leisure class.

Right Mrs. Robinson was the original cougar in part, at least, because of her chic, seductive wardrobe. Costume designer Patricia Zipprodt dressed Anne Bancroft in sheer, silky blacks and tactile leopard prints in order to prove that a woman's animal instincts are ageless.

With her skins and streaks, pencil skirts and lace, Mrs. Robinson might as well have been dressed by Dolce and Gabbana.

Mia Farrow embodied the new youthfulness and sexy androgyny that swept the world in the 1960s. Her boyish shape and pixie haircut could give even the most feminine dress—like the pleated and adorned silk chiffon number shown here—an unexpected, slightly transgressive edge.

< Benjamin falls for Elaine immediately. Her innocence trumps her mother's experience. The rest of the movie chronicles Benjamin's effort to win Elaine's heart, a difficult prospect considering she knows that he has slept with her mother. As we track her running around the Berkeley campus in straightforward, neutral pantsuits that befit a revolution, we're meant to fall more and more in love with Elaine's innocence and her lack of artifice. Her mother, meanwhile, disintegrates into a jealous, alcoholic lump of smeared mascara and crow's feet.

It's not really much of a surprise at the end of the movie when Benjamin and his Berkeley princess ride off into the rest of their lives slumped in the back of a public bus: she in her wedding dress, he in a polo shirt, disheveled windbreaker, and dirty white jeans. The haunting, down-tempo music by Simon and Garfunkel takes us out of the story and into their uncertain future. Whatever fate awaits these innocents, it's certain that Mrs. Robinson, abandoned, will end up drunk and alone on a chaise in her perfect house, watching the revolution on TV.

Over forty years later, Mrs. Robinson's —not Elaine's—is the image that endures. But in 1967, when the movie was released, the Mrs. Robinsons of the world were already out of fashion. Society was experiencing the most extreme and exhilarating social change that it had seen since the 1920s,

and a pillbox hat wouldn't exactly have been the most practical headgear for a riot.

The sixties were the decade that finally took fashion out of the designer's sketchbook and turned it into a mirror of popular culture. It was about the runaways, not the runways. Womanly was out; girlie was in. The ideal silhouette was giant head floating atop skewer body.

The models of the moment were gamine sprites, not paragons of femininity. Frank Sinatra moved from Ava Gardner, she of the legendary D-cups, to Mia Farrow, a pixie in a baby-doll dress. Twiggy, who lived up to her name, became an international beauty icon. Goldie Hawn took up where Doris Day left off as America's comic sweetheart. European film starlets were no longer Fellini fertility goddesses, but the sneakers-and-stripes-wearing tomboys favored by Godard. Mary Quant, André Courrèges, and Pierre Cardin sold skirts so short they verged on vulgar. The bodies of the girls who wore them, though, were so starved of their womanly attributes that they couldn't have looked vulgar if they tried. Instead, they looked like aerodynamic space lollipops sailing toward the future at the speed of light.

Vitti wore simple silhouettes in mostly black and white, but there was something utterly nontraditional about her.

Monica/Peggy

Monica Vitti was the muse to Italian director Michelangelo Antonioni. Feminine as a 1950s Fellini starlet, Vitti wore simple silhouettes in mostly black and white, but there was something utterly nontraditional about her. She was the personification of the minimalist, sensual, and somehow deeply tragic aesthetic of Antonioni's highly artistic shooting style.

Peggy Moffitt was a youthful coquette with perfect breasts, Vidal-Sasson coiffure and cheeky attitude, whose collaboration with Austrian-born L.A. designer Rudi Gernreich elevated his racy designs to the status of high art. More than any other model before or since, Moffitt had a singular appeal that taught the mainstream to appreciate unconventional beauty. Although she fits into the boyish group of women who came to redefine femininity through the mod, pop, and space-age aesthetics, Moffitt's appeal transcends trend because of the intelligence she brought to every picture she appeared in. Where teenage models were little more than oxygen-consuming rag dolls, Moffitt was an intense and kinetic force to be reckoned with.

Vitti and Moffitt represent the two aesthetic periods of the 1960s. The first —represented by Vitti—was epitomized by women who, despite their simple, elegant daywear, projected a dense aura of mystery born of a vast and complicated

life experience. Antonioni's Italians bubbled with sexuality, while Hitchcock's Nordic princesses were covered in a layer of ice. Monochromatic day suits, swing coats, sensible walking heels, a perfectly set coiffure, flawless eyeliner—on the outside, these women were idealized versions of femininity, projections of ultimate male desire, but inside, something much more complex simmered under the traditional allure.

The second aesthetic period of the decade—represented by Moffitt—was a result of the sort of trauma and upheaval of which history had never seen. Teenage daughters, not their well-coiffed mothers, began to set the styles. Androgynous, fearless, iconoclastic: The new girl wore miniskirts and go-go boots, baby-doll dresses and topless bathing suits. In the wake of the assassinations of President Kennedy and Dr. King, in the shadow of the Vietnam War, sporting a coordinated couture ensemble made a gal look out of touch with what was going on in the world. High-fashion designers were forced to reinvent their sources of inspiration in order to stay relevant. The sixties were the first decade in which "street" fashion truly informed haute couture.

Dressed in a boyish blazer and button-down, with her hair pulled back, Monica Vitti oozes a cool, rebellious sex appeal which must have seemed quite *modern* in March 1965. Vitti was unconventional offscreen, too, living "in sin" with her partner Roberto Russo for twenty years before marrying him.

Above Peggy Moffitt was the sort of woman more likely to have checkers played upon her than to play checkers herself. Her plunging graphic check tunic is worn belted, with matching stockings, block earrings, and loafers.

Right In 1967, Designer Rudi Gernreich gives the once-over to his longtime muse, Peggy Moffitt, who wears a four-piece colorblock ensemble comprised of a piped bikini and knee pads.

At the beginning of the sixties, the titans of tailoring were still turning out magnificent creations at home in the previous decade's polished world. French haute couture designer Pierre Balmain brought the elegance and ornamentation of impeccable fifties couture to the slimmer, more abbreviated shapes of the sixties. Even though his gowns boasted old-fashioned couture techniques, most notably the Lesage embroidery that had long been a hallmark of a top-notch piece of evening wear, they lacked the volume that was the sometimes-dated signature of the postwar decade.

Jacqueline Kennedy was known to be the belle of the ball in a Balmain on occasion, but her real loyalty was to Oleg Cassini, whom the White House chose to be her official Svengali for her tenure as first lady. Many were surprised when Cassini was chosen over better-known couturiers, but his low-key, aristocratic persona—he was the son of the Russian ambassador to the United States and an Italian countess—meant that he understood the needs of a woman who had to inspire, not overwhelm. Cassini was the man who made the square jacket, pillbox hat, and satin gown into the hallmarks of demure style in the first half of the decade.

Ferdinand Sarmi was the Republican Cassini. An Italian with a similar aesthetic and clientele, but less notoriety, Sarmi began his career as the head designer for cosmetics queen Elizabeth Arden's fledgling couture house in New York, where he designed Pat Nixon's inauguration gown in 1957. When Arden and Sarmi locked horns—she reportedly took to the bows on her gowns with scissors, saying that they needed to represent her brand, not his—he struck out on his own, and maintained his client base of fashionable wives and debutantes. A Sarmi creation was the perfect choice for those who wanted to be impeccable but not overwhelming, combining old-school grace with a liberal—okay, conservative—dash of sparkle. >

Old Age/Space Age

Left Wearing navy silk Donald Brooks and carrying a chic little firearm, this woman is dressed to kill—literally.

Overleaf Jacqueline Kennedy Onassis leaving the London airport by car in November 1968. Her husband, Aristotle Onassis, is just visible in the front seat.

< The man who perfected the art of using old-school decoration techniques on slimmed-down silhouettes was Norman Norell, an American. The poufy party frocks he produced for his collaborative line, Traina-Norell, in the fifties were replaced by the otherworldly mermaid gowns that became his trademark and legacy. Made of silk jersey and painstakingly covered in metallic paillettes, these jewel-toned love letters to the female form were at once dazzling odes to thirties glamour and glimpses into the future of eighties glitz.

Working at the opposite end of the social spectrum from the designers who catered to the ladies who lunched were the movers and shakers starting a youthquake in Europe.

British designer Mary Quant's streamlined aesthetic was based on movement. From dance tights to soccer uniforms, her design inspirations came from a world where young and able bodies were always in motion. Quant was the high priestess of the mod movement, and she is widely credited with inventing the miniskirt. Although that honor may actually be due to French designer André Courrèges, there's no question that Quant and her disciples— supermodels Twiggy, Jean Shrimpton, and Peggy Moffitt among them—had everything to do with making the world go wild for it. They were frolicking about in a high-style romper room, dressed in frocks that could have been stolen off the racks at primary school. >

Mod fashion of the 1960s was a study in geometry. Here, the lines and rectangles that compose the model's dress both contrast with and complement the orbs and ovals of her beehive . . .

Little Lady Fauntleroy. In a photograph from 1967, Twiggy lounges on a chair designed by Le Corbusier, wearing a metal mesh vest by Roberto Rojas and tights by Rudi Gernreich. Her watch is by Sig Prager for Schiaparelli and is attached to her wrist with gold handchains.

Below A model wears a striped sequined Biba ensemble, in January 1969. Biba was the British boutique chain where gorgeous mod girls went to score their getups. Even though their styles were doll-like and their fabrics were granny-licious, Biba dresses covered the backs of the prettiest party girls in Swingin' London.

Right A trio of models wearing Betsey Johnson for Paraphernalia minidresses and opaque tights by Solar, in 1966.

< Courrèges, who was saving as many francs in fabric yardage as Quant was saving pounds sterling, was more interested in space camp than day care. Where Quant's clothes from 1964 are deliberately infantile, Courrèges's are futuristic. Having trained for ten years under Balenciaga, Courrèges was interested in engaging in the intellectual side of fashion, using the languages of geometry and color to elevate women into another world. His short dresses, usually in A-line shift shapes, with patch pockets, were made of heavy, stiff fabrics in order to hold their structure, but they weren't restrictive. Where Quant's miniskirts were social, encouraging women to move freely, Courrèges' were conceptual, encouraging them to think freely.

Paco Rabanne, a Basque designer based in Paris, also worked with Balenciaga—but as a jewelry designer. Combined with his formal architect's training, Rabanne's familiarity with hard materials such as plastic and metal allowed him to come up with a completely one-of-a-kind interpretation of the miniskirt trend. He created what was essentially body jewelry, "knitting" metals and interlocking plastic disks to form materials that turned the skin's surface into the background of an intricately decorated fabric. Perhaps Rabanne's best-known accomplishment is designing Jane Fonda's many costumes for *Barbarella*; he put the sexy in space age.

The last of the European mini-masters was Pierre Cardin. Like Courrèges and Rabanne,

Cardin had an impressive pedigree. He worked with Paquin, Schiaparelli, and Dior before starting his own house. Where his contemporaries were interested in putting a woman's body on display for its own sake, Cardin used the body as a foundation on which to build his often-outlandish creations. Like Schiaparelli's, Cardin's zanier works captured the public's attention and made them think about the crossover between fashion and avant-garde art. But also like Schiaparelli, Cardin had a somewhat hidden gift for coming up with subdued, elegant pieces with as much function as flamboyance. Details such as a sweet quilted bib on a simple shift dress, or dramatic silver collar and cuffs on a streamlined black maxi, made his best creations at once the most wearable and most special items in a woman's closet.

Below To create this coat, designer Paco Rabanne nailed together triangular panels of leather to mimic the look of chain mail.

Right Five models sporting a rainbow of Pierre Cardin dresses in 1965. Cardin was known for cheerful, accessible daywear more than exorbitant evening looks, but he didn't mind being out of the "high-fashion" in-crowd: "They said prêt-a-porter will kill your name," he mused, "and it saved me."

American cultural history breaks the sixties down into two periods: before and after JFK was assassinated. The Camelot years were characterized by images of sheer perfection. Even though some of the Kennedy administration's ideas were quite socially liberal, they were presented in a pretty package that was palatable to even the most old-fashioned Americans. Kennedy was the president who sought to change the world while still playing by the rules. When his promise was extinguished, nobody cared about the rules anymore. In the primordial soup cooked up by grief, hopelessness, anger, and action came an aesthetic free-for-all, and debutantes were turning into Factory Girls left and right. History didn't matter—the old regime had made a mess of things. Pop art was rewriting the language of style.

Art critic George Melly, in his book *Revolt into Style*, wrote, "Pop has imposed the idea of instant success based on the promotion of a personal style rather than a search for content or meaning." This new generation of style makers was obsessed with being documented purely for the sake of vanity and fame. In an early scene in *Blow-Up*, Antonioni's first English-language film, supermodel Verushka poses for a fashion photographer played by David Hemmings. The two relate to each other as though they are having sex—through intimate eye contact and body language—and their mutual climax is achieved through taking the perfect picture. Once this act is complete, they are fulfilled, finding pure pleasure in the making of a perfect image.

Of course, the cool kids also found pleasure in doing drugs. Pot, psychedelics, pills, heroin—people were opening their minds, literally, and the way the world looked was changing. Doping was no longer about demure, doctor-prescribed downers—they went out with Marilyn Monroe in 1962. Now the cool kids wanted to speed things up and expand their consciousness. The use of amphetamines, LSD, and marijuana led to a new spirit of creativity in fashion. The archetypal university student was no longer the preppy Harvard Brahmin but the shaggy Berkeley drum-circler. College kids traded wardrobe elements handed down by the leisure class—navy blazers, khaki pants, Oxford shirts—for radical, subversive ones that came straight out of the military: jumpsuits, uniform jackets, machine guns (paging Patty Hearst and Hanoi Jane). >

A still from Michelangelo Antonioni's *Blow-Up*, which was *the* fashion movie of 1966. The film featured a slew of top models acting as . . . top models.

Pillbox Hats/**Pills**

Debutantes were turning into Factory Girls left and right. Pop art was rewriting the language of style.

Where they doused their bodies in patchouli, Sedgwick dipped hers in glitter.

< Edie Sedgwick was the poster child for this newly liberal generation of American haves. Like her counterparts in San Francisco and Laurel Canyon, New Yorker Sedgwick brought a playful, rule-breaking spirit to her wardrobe. But where they were stepping into burnt-orange cords, she was pulling on black tights. Where they doused their bodies in patchouli, she dipped hers in glitter. Where they took LSD, she took speed.

Sedgwick's signature style was based largely on her desire to function as a twin to her male Svengali, Andy Warhol. Sadly, much of the courage and freedom she needed to transform herself from debutante to performance artist was found first in a prescription bottle, then in a syringe. Eventually, she ended up a product of the Warhol factory, flat as a Warhol silk-screen portrait. Of course, that was likely Warhol's vision for her all along.

Left Work by the American Pop artist Tom Wesselmann inspired these long-sleeved shift dresses by Yves Saint Laurent, photographed in Paris in 1966. The dress on the left featured a black-and-white eye and red lips appliquéd onto a deep purple background, while the one on the right was described as a "silhouette voluptueuse."

Above It Girl Edie Sedgwick at a party with Andy Warhol in the sixties. "Fashion as a whole is a farce, completely," she once said. "The people behind it are perverted, the styles are created by freaked out people, just natural weirdos. I know this because I worked with all those people while I was modeling."

As the drug culture in the United States and Europe racked up a long list of casualties, those still interested in pushing the boundaries of consciousness—mainly rock stars, playboys, and the women who loved them—journeyed east. While at the beginning of the decade, the rock 'n' roll aesthetic was about mod, by the time Talitha and J. Paul Getty decamped to Marrakech in the late sixties, the world of style was spearheading its own spice trade. Caftans, djellabas, and dashikis found a place in Western wardrobes. Although the styles derived from different cultures varied wildly, they emanated a common aura—and it smelled of marijuana and opium. Those who wore these totems of exotica communicated a certain worldliness and spirit of adventure that was often associated with recreational drug use at the time.

Ossie Clark was a dashing young bloke who partied like a rock star—because with names like Mick, Keith, Jimi, John, and Paul, his friends *were* rock stars. In his travels through London nightlife, Clark met many of the women whose candid party pictures would become his label's best advertisements. Bianca Jagger was married in an Ossie Clark original cheekily designed to allow wedding guests a glimpse of her nipples. Twiggy showed off his clothes in *Vogue*, commissioning

one-of-a-kind pieces for her own personal collection. Marianne Faithfull, the original Band-Aid, was often seen in—and sometimes out—of a Clark. "Ossie wanted everything to be on bare skin, so he said, 'Take it all off,' and I did," Faithfull told the *New York Times*. "I remember a lot of the dresses— they were so wonderful to wear . . . It was about being young. We had time, leisure and money enough. It all added up to a very sensual atmosphere."

Clark wasn't all flash. His designs were at once innovative and classical. "Ossie Clark captured the perfect mix between sexuality and femininity," commented Stella McCartney in the brochure for his retrospective exhibition at the Warrington Museum and Art Gallery. He perfected the art of constructing a dress cut on the bias—John Galliano will be forever in Clark's debt—using crepe to create luxuriously draped confections. Clark's vivid, floral-print collaborations with his textile designer wife, Celia Birtwell, are well known for the harmony they achieve between print and cut, but many of his most enduring pieces were made from plain fabrics that allowed their shapes to take center stage. >

Rock the Boat/
Rock the Casbah

J. Paul Getty and his wife, Talitha, on the patio of their home in Marrakech. They combined pioneer spirits, wanderlust, and impeccable taste to define what we think of as bohemian chic.

< Even though he had a true signature aesthetic, and pioneered many design innovations, when Clark spoke about his work, he made a point of not taking himself too seriously as an artist. He told the *New York Times* that, for the women he dressed, "the clothes weren't that important. It was a whole attitude. It was about taking off their bras and enjoying themselves."

Another Brit responsible for shaking a dash of spice into the wardrobes of well-heeled Westerners was Thea Porter. Porter's fondness for exoticism grew out of her own upbringing. Born to British and French parents in Palestine in 1927, she was raised in Damascus in a missionary family.

Porter dressed Anglo women in lush getups more suited to a night in with a maharaja than a night out on the town. Although she dressed everyone from Elizabeth Taylor and Jane Fonda to society matron Jayne Wrightsman and the Begum Aga Khan, Porter's effort to expand her label beyond lavish couture and into the realm of mainstream ready-to-wear was unsuccessful, maybe because in order to pull off a jewel-encrusted floor-length caftan, one had better have a ball to wear it to. (And a good ball was getting harder and harder to come by.)

Porter dressed Anglo women in lush getups more suited to a night in with a maharaja than a night out on the town.

The colors of this Thea Porter ensemble featured in British *Vogue*, 1969, may be red, white and blue, but its vibe is exotic, not patriotic. Bringing the Middle East out west, Porter catered to a posh clientele who demanded the most luxurious silhouettes fashioned from the most lavish fabrics.

Beyond the lollipop vision of mod and space age lay the androgynous, utopian realm of Rudi Gernreich. Austrian-born, the openly gay Gernreich fled the Nazis and came to Los Angeles as a dancer, reinventing himself as a fashion designer in the fifties. Gernreich's racy creations—the most famous of which were swimsuits that revealed parts of the body no designer had dared expose before—were mod in shape and color, but brazen in attitude. Acutely interested in identity politics, Gernreich managed, paradoxically, to uncover the body by covering it. Women looked more naked in his clothing than they did completely nude.

Gernreich found fame at the turn of the decade, when the legendary Diana Vreeland, then editor of *Harper's Bazaar*, fell in love with a line of wool swimsuits he designed for Westwood Knitting Mills. Instead of squeezing and lifting the curves of a woman's body into submission, they simply revealed its true form.

In 1964, he went a step—or, rather, a giant leap—further, unveiling the breasts entirely in the design of his topless swimsuit. Once again, Vreeland, now at *Vogue*, was a strong and vocal supporter. The controversial suit garnered enough press coverage to rival the moon landing, with the *New York Times*, the *Saturday Evening Post*, the *Los Angeles Herald Examiner*, and others reporting on the moral outrage that resulted from the introduction of the iconoclastic garment. It was officially banned by the pope. Still, according to Peggy Moffitt (see page 134), those who interpreted it as sexualized were missing the point: "The suit is . . . about freedom and not display," she said.

And Moffitt's statement was true of all Gernreich's clothes, from his tube dresses to vinyl decals, "Ringo" suits to trompe l'oeil knits. Gernreich understood that fashion power was shifting from wealth to youth, from the ballrooms to the street. In 1967, along with his spring collection, he presented a mission statement of sorts: "For the first time in the history of the world—at least since the Children's Crusade—the young are leading us . . . They are discovering their fashion power just as they are discovering their social and political power. They are bringing about a natural fusion of person and dress. And what is amusing is that the older people are beginning to revolt." By this time, technically, Gernreich, at forty-five, was one of these "older people." But he didn't design like it.

DESIGNER OF THE DECADE

Rudi Gernreich

A major departure from his usually mod, futuristic looks, these flouncy polka-dotted creations from Rudi Gernreich might seem out of character. But with their outlandish color combinations and their sheer joie de vivre, the spirit of these getups is vintage Gernreich.

The 1970s

In *Annie Hall*, Woody Allen's masterpiece from 1977, actress Diane Keaton looks effortlessly cool in a men's button-down shirt with a tailored vest and a polka-dot tie. Combining teenage-babysitter hair with Grandpa's khakis doesn't seem like the recipe for a fashion icon, but that's exactly what the character of Annie Hall became. Annie's style was based on Keaton's: When she came in to audition, the director was captivated by the way she dressed. The film's costume designer told Allen that Keaton's eccentric style would be off-putting to viewers, but Allen resisted pressure to glamify Annie, and thank goodness he did. Her quirky androgyny makes her positively emblematic of the 1970s. Annie's style represents risk taking, humor, and an inversion of traditional sexuality that turns Fashion (capital "F" intentional) on its head.

In his charming and bizarre memoir *Growing (Up) at 37*, social activist Jerry Rubin characterized the flower children as the first generation to reincarnate themselves during the course of their own lifetimes. Rubin himself went from storming the streets as a violent revolutionary—one of the Chicago Seven—to being BFFs with self-help guru Werner Erhard, of "est" fame. One of the funny things about the sixties is that while most young people thought they were striking out boldly on their own, everybody was really doing pretty much the same thing by acting "anti-establishment." You've seen one daisy chain, you've seen 'em all. If the sixties were about banding together into one common identity in the service of social change, then the seventies were about the quest to venture out in search of a truly authentic self. And that, of course, meant a new wardrobe.

Discovering that wardrobe entailed embarking on a hunt through an enchanted forest of disparate trends, where a person could pluck a djellaba from one tree and a pair of skinny jeans from another. The goal in the seventies was to look like no one other than yourself. Those who lived and shopped the seventies witnessed a number of important evolutions; fashion moved from natural to synthetic, handmade to machine-made, folk to punk, crochet to lamé. And unlike in previous decades, when a fashion girl was expected to abandon her favorite outfit du jour and move on to the next complete look, a seventies fashion plate didn't have to say goodbye to her favorite pieces once the next thing came along. She kept collecting items in the hopes of turning her closet into a giant, one-of-a-kind collage. And if one day she felt like piling every single piece on at once, no one would look at her cross-eyed. In the sixties, magazines were still giving hemline orders and women obeyed. In the seventies, a woman became the fashion director of her own closet.

Previous Detail of a ruched strapless gown designed by James Galanos in the 1970s. Even though his dresses were technically considered ready-to-wear rather than couture, each and every pleat and pinch was attended to by hand in order to meet the standards of high-profile clients such as Nancy Reagan, Elizabeth Taylor, Diana Ross, Betsy Bloomingdale, and Rosalind Russell.

Right In this Norman Parkinson photo taken in 1971 and featured in the September issue of British *Vogue*, model Nicky Samuel wears an Ossie Clark dress featuring a print by Celia Birtwell. Samuel was married to Nigel Waymouth, proprietor of *Granny Takes a Trip*, a psychedelic-glam boutique on the King's Road in London. The print orgy shown here harkens back to the Pre-Raphaelite movement.

Taken in 1975, this seaside image of a cotton kimono shows the profound influence of Eastern textiles—in this case, specifically Japanese—on Western fashion.

No one directed her own closet with more fashion confidence than Bianca Jagger, lover and wife of Mick, fantasy lovechild of Eva Perón and David Bowie. Her fearless, Latin American glamour had a dangerous and exhilarating sense of freedom about it. She took some serious fashion risks—we're talking feathered headdresses, lariats, and walking sticks here—but because of her feline poise, Jagger's wild getups never wore her. Even though she wasn't selling anything, she crafted an impeccable personal brand sheerly by instinct. And her instinct was to only come out at night.

Ultimate supermodel Cheryl Tiegs was like the mirror image of Jagger; not simply for obvious reasons, but also because Tiegs seemed to be a physical manifestation of male fantasy, whereas Jagger was a creature of her own creation. Tiegs exemplified what men wanted as well as what women wanted to be. With her beaming disposition, her athletic grace, and the complexion of a newborn, Tiegs was like a human can of SunnyDelight juice concentrate.

Tiegs and Jagger exemplify the poles of the 1970s sexual ideal: athletic, daytime magnetism on one side; mysterious, disco sensuality on the other. Still, their unapologetic emphasis on the body and utterly ubiquitous presence in the media made them the faces—and bodies—of the decade.

Right Relaxing at her home in Chelsea, London, Bianca Jagger wears a voluminous yellow robe by British designer Zandra Rhodes. Despite her slight frame, she put on—and pulled off—clothes that boasted vast swathes of fabric. Jagger was no stranger to drama: She entered her thirtieth birthday celebration wearing a hooded Halston gown, and riding on a white horse.

Overleaf, left With her blond hair, blue eyes, and feminine-yet-athletic figure, Cheryl Tiegs may have risen to fame in swimsuits, snagging no fewer than three *Sports Illustrated* covers in a decade, but she also had the knack for high fashion.

Overleaf, right Wearing one of her signature fitted white tuxedo jackets, and a jaunty fur stole, Bianca Jagger attends a press conference in Munich in the early eighties.

Bianca/Cheryl

Tiegs and Jagger exemplify the poles of the 1970s sexual ideal: athletic, daytime magnetism on one side; mysterious, disco sensuality on the other.

Of the many prostitutes that abound in seventies films, the most memorable ones are—gasp!—children. Think Jodi Foster in *Taxi Driver* (1976), or Brooke Shields in *Pretty Baby* (1978). Unlike the way we might imagine a child prostitute today—a vision in spandex, perhaps, with a fondness for lip plumpers and straightening irons— these girls actually looked like girls, with their wholesome wardrobes, rosy cheeks, Cupid's bow lips, and pin-curled hair. Floral prints, natural fibers, wide-brimmed hats, puffy sleeves: All the visual trademarks of a well-bred baby doll were found on the most taboo of sex objects in the seventies.

Of course the seventies offered another visual expression of sexuality, too: the what-you-see-is-what-you-get glitter and gloss of disco. Where *Taxi Driver* and *Pretty Baby* fetishized images of bohemian innocence, *Saturday Night Fever* (1977) employed body-skimming synthetic fabrics, low necklines, and a liberal use of flash to draw attention to the body's naughty bits. Grown women wore rompers and playsuits. And romp and play they did!

The hypersexualized blow-up doll on one hand and the demure baby doll on the other are the two poles of female sexuality that characterized most of the dressy looks of the seventies. On one end of the spectrum were underage hookers and cosseted housewives in Victorian-inspired floral maxi-dresses, and on the other were satin-skinned beauties such as Bianca Jagger and Margaux Hemingway, tearing up the dance floor at Studio 54. The furthest thing from a disco getup was a floor-length gown made of white lace, but in the zany seventies, the two were equally fashionable. It was the decade of expression versus repression.

British designer Laura Ashley was at least in part responsible for starting the maxi-dress craze. Ashley was raised a strict Baptist in her native England, so the modest nature of her designs isn't really surprising. Still, despite the lack of visible skin on a woman cloaked in Ashley, the creations exuded a simmering sensuality for all they *didn't* reveal. By the middle of the decade, this covered-up look had been immortalized in the cult classic *The Stepford Wives*. It seemed the only women who could stand to stay hidden like this were robots. (And men, of course, found that hot.)

In contrast to the prairie-chic sensibility calico maxis espoused, the jersey dance dresses favored by denizens of Studio 54 and Regine's were streamlined, stretchy, and seemed to whisper "sexsexsex." The chief purveyor of these figure-skimming confections was Roy Halston Frowick, fashion minister to the rich, famous, and fabulous. >

Libertines/
New Victorians

Left Jodie Foster in character as a twelve-year-old prostitute from the 1976 film *Taxi Driver*.

Above Margaux Hemingway at the Beverly Hills Hotel in 1975, wearing a white off-the-shoulder top and skirt by John Anthony.

Overleaf This 1979 advertisement for Charles Jourdan was shot by Guy Bourdin, a fashion photographer who was underappreciated in his time, but found fame after his death in the early 1990s. In a profile for the *New Yorker*, Anthony Haden-Guest wrote that Bourdin "managed to imbue photographs intended for selling clothing, cosmetics, and perfume with the preternatural vividness of dreams." Clearly, this model is dreaming about John Travolta.

Because Halston's creations depended heavily on the bias cut, they swayed and moved in time to the beat of the disco music.

Left Beverly Johnson was the first African-American model to appear on the cover of *Vogue* (in August 1974). In spite of its pastel palette, the Halston gown Johnson wears here showcases the drama and movement that were his hallmarks.

Overleaf From Helmut Newton to Guy Bourdin, fashion photography in the seventies was all about girl-on-girl psychosexual melodrama. In the service of selling sequins and stilettos, women were allowed to explore their darkest sides in public.

< Halston's designs varied from diaphanous and playful to drapey and dramatic, but always owed a huge debt to the original mistress of draping, Madame Vionnet (see page 38). Because his creations, like Vionnet's, depended heavily on the bias cut, they swayed and moved in time to the beat of the disco music.

It's important to note that not all ladies dressed like women of the night—some, in fact, dressed like the men who ran their schedules. At the risk of being indelicate, there were hos—and there were pimps. The slim, meticulously tailored pantsuit was often the most subversive option in a sea of femininity. Not only John Lennon but also Yoko Ono commissioned bespoke suits from Savile Row tailor Tommy Nutter, who pioneered the long, slim lines and glovelike fit to which Tom Ford and Stella McCartney would later pay tribute. An Yves Saint Laurent tuxedo continued to be a chic alternative to the evening gown, as it had been ever since its inception in the late sixties.

At the same time women were dressing like men, men were dressing like women. A quick glance around any New York, London, or L.A. dance floor proved that some of the most glamorous "women" of the seventies weren't technically women at all. David Bowie as Ziggy Stardust—with his sky-scraping platforms, his clingy, sparkling separates, and a full face of Mary Kay—is frequently given sole credit for the trend in cross-dressing

moving beyond drag clubs, but the glam rock look bubbled up from the streets and was at least as much a product of Warhol's Factory as of Bowie's album cover.

The seventies marked the first period of time since Weimar Berlin that an androgynous look was so widely accepted in the mass culture. This reversal of gender roles was probably the most groundbreaking and enduring legacy of the time, because it greatly broadened the variety of wardrobe options available to both sexes and blasted away scores of social taboos.

The man responsible for originating the Ziggy Stardust look was Kansai Yamamoto, who brought the influence of his Japanese heritage to his designs and paved the way for a bevy of influential countrymen to rock fashion in the coming decades. In 1973, Yamamoto said of Bowie, "He has an unusual face, don't you think? He's neither man nor woman, if you see what I mean; which suited me as a designer because most of my clothes are for either sex." Anyone familiar with the ancient art of Kabuki theater knows that masquerade has long been socially sanctioned in Japan. This *other* Yamamoto—who arrived on the scene long before Yohji—translated all the visual totems of that practice into the language of arena rock. Kimono shapes, MENSA-level construction, and intricate appliqués were all hallmarks of Ziggy's style and have remained key techniques in high and low fashion ever since.

DESIGNER OF THE DECADE

Yves Saint Laurent

Though Yves Saint Laurent consistently produced iconic collections over the course of five decades—from the fifties through the nineties—his seventies looks really represent the distillation of his aesthetic. In the summer of 1971, Saint Laurent arrived at a place that feminists wouldn't reach until decades later: empowering women through sophistication. He presented a collection that made risky visual references to the Second World War as an antidote to an excess of flower power. Real, ladylike outfits—high heels, seductive daytime dresses—looked more revolutionary than the denim bell-bottoms the revolutionaries wore. In the 1940s, women were strong because they had to be. Saint Laurent didn't shy away from ambiguity—he ran toward it. It wasn't enough just to pose the question; he also tried to provide the answer.

"My dream is to give women the basis for a classic wardrobe, which, while escaping the fashion of the moment, will give them greater confidence in themselves," he said. Saint Laurent combined the sophistication and craftsmanship of haute couture with the innovation of street style and the richness of exotic cultures, forever changing the way fashionable women dressed.

And unlike the other great couturiers who came before him, Saint Laurent was not interested in playing the role of Pygmalion.

"If one tries to impose one's own interests, one's own fantasies, ahead of those of women, one ends up with disguises," he once said. Instead of using women as canvases, he translated his interests and inspirations into pieces that were at once modern and timeless, and that always aimed to put a woman's beauty and personality into focus. Whether he was crafting an ode to the color palette of Marrakech or the androgyny of Weimar Berlin, Saint Laurent brought effortless wearability to the most outlandish of inspirations.

The Ballets Russes collection that Saint Laurent presented in 1976 was revolutionary, but not in a proletarian way. Inspired by the same eclectic dance company as Paul Poiret had been in the 1910s (see page 44), not only did he take the looks themselves over the top—with luxurious embroidery, decadent fur, voluminous sleeves, and layers and layers of silk—but he also turned the showcasing of these looks into a true spectacle. From then on, a "fashion show" was no longer a staid presentation of couture to potential buyers, but an extravaganza, a production, a full bells-and-whistles Show. It brought proud glamour back to an industry that had loosened up significantly—perhaps too much—since the sixties. He brought age-old trademarks of the aristocracy to the cutting edge of fashion, and dared women to be brave—and rich—enough to wear them.

Overleaf, left Norman Parkinson's street photograph, taken in 1973, captures the effortlessness and insouciance of Yves Saint Laurent's iconic women's tuxedo design, "Le Smoking."

Above The exotic-erotic feel of Yves Saint Laurent's breakthrough Ballets Russes collection of 1976 foreshadowed the vibe of his wildly popular fragrance, Opium, which was introduced the following year.

Overleaf, right In this Norman Parkinson photograph from 1975, a very young Jerry Hall—eighties supermodel and the second Mrs. Jagger—wears a deep burgundy caftan by Yves Saint Laurent.

The 1980s

In *The Pick-up Artist*, one of many delightful romantic comedies made in the golden age of teen cinema, Molly Ringwald says to Robert Downey Jr., who is, of course, trying to pick her up: "Your line is that you have no line." Replace "line" with "style" and the same phrase can be used to describe the look of the eighties. The style was that we had no style. And by that I don't mean we weren't stylish; it's that our fashion identities kept changing.

In the eighties, when I was working at L.A.'s glamour hotbed, Theodore, my friends and I were all shape-shifters. We wanted to come across as insouciant individualists—flouting convention by shopping for 1950s cowboy shirts in a Venice thrift shop one day, then at Bijan for a linen blazer the next—but what we were really doing was trend-hopping—jumping from zeitgeist to zeitgeist instead of cultivating a signature style. Consistency wasn't key—conspicuous consumption was. And for clothing manufacturers, this meant a whole new way of doing business.

Until the eighties, American fashion had really taken a backseat to European, in terms of global influence. According to Fern Mallis, the creator of New York Fashion Week, until American designers began to showcase their work in an organized fashion (week)—as the Europeans had been doing for decades—their ideas went largely unnoticed by the rest of the world. While European designers needed to sell their lines in the United States in order to stay afloat financially, the Americans had enough customers stateside to keep them occupied. They were seen more as following fashion than setting it. But once superstar designers like Donna Karan and Calvin Klein had a global platform, American fashion finally became a vital part of the international conversation, and ideas bounced back and forth like Super Balls, from New York to London, Tokyo to Milan.

Also changing the game in the eighties was the rise to power of street fashion. Because of the proliferation of fashion in media, from MTV music videos to *Style with Elsa Klench*, trends were bubbling up, not just trickling down. From Studio 54 to the King's Road, Run DMC's sneakers to Debbie Harry's unitards, the runway commenced a vibrant dialogue with the real world that's still going strong today.

Signature looks of the eighties are preserved not just on celebrities in video stills but also on civilians in party pictures. Scores of meticulously constructed, often outlandish, always over-the-top frocks—out of place anywhere but a celebration and worn by mothers and daughters alike—made the eighties the decade of the party dress, and today's style-setters remain obsessed with dropped-waist taffeta and one-shouldered chiffon, slinky chemises and poufy bubble skirts—all totems of eighties Dionysian excess. These reappearances probably have something to do with the many socioeconomic parallels between the eighties and the oughts—will everyone, past, present, and future, always want to party like it's 1999?—but as with all styles that endure, their power must also be driven by pure aesthetics.

Previous A Christian Lacroix for Jean Patou Haute Couture corseted gown in silk taffeta from 1987. The *New York Times* credited Patou's "daffy but amusing approach" to fashion with "reviving" couture, citing his "astonishing" sense of whimsy and juxtaposition. But they failed to mention his knack for creating serious sex appeal, even underneath yards and yards of stiff fabric (and reputation).

Right The eighties were not about traveling light, but traveling right. Exhibit A: Supermodel Kelly Emberg in New York in 1982, en route to the friendly skies clad in a blue gabardine suit by Calvin Klein, with luggage by Lancel, Mark Cross, and Chanel in tow.

Overleaf The present staring down the past: Wearing a 1987 creation designed by Marc Bohan for Christian Dior, a model looks down her nose at Dior, version one—a New Look ensemble from forty years earlier. Bohan took the helm at Dior in 1960, when Yves Saint Laurent left to start his own label.

From Studio 54 to the King's Road, the runway commenced a vibrant dialogue with the real world.

Andy Warhol's portrait of Tina Chow, made in 1985. She credited Warhol with inspiring her career as a jewelry designer when he gave her a piece of aquamarine crystal.

Tina/Debbie

Neither Tina Chow nor Debbie Harry ever fell prey to the bloated hair, makeup, and shoulder pads that defined the decade's "bad" fashion. Both of these women could walk the streets of downtown New York today, wearing any one of their outfits from 1981, and still look enviably chic, even fashion-forward.

Born Bettina Lutz in 1951, the daughter of an American GI and a Japanese woman who met during the American occupation of Japan, Tina Chow had a serene yet mysterious androgyny that made her an internationally accomplished fashion model by the age of sixteen. An Ohio native, she encountered prejudice as a Japanese American born shortly after the Second World War. She claimed never to have been asked out on a date—or even to dance—while still living in cheerleader-obsessed Ohio.

Tina moved to Tokyo with her parents when she was a teenager, and started her career modeling for the cosmetics company Shiseido. Soon she began to walk runways—she did Issey Miyake's very first show—and pose for magazines. Legendary photographers Cecil Beaton, Helmut Newton, and Herb Ritts—three of the business's least easily impressed—went crazy over her heart-shaped face and ambiguous ethnicity.

Tina was introduced to her husband, restaurateur Michael Chow, by the fashion designer Zandra Rhodes in 1971. "She was a match that lights some things and makes them burn brighter," Rhodes told *New York* magazine shortly after Tina died at the age of 41, in 1992. "She was an attractive, elegant instigator." Two years after they met, Tina and Michael were married at his London restaurant, which was called Mr. Chow, in the company of rock and screen stars. Shoe designer Manolo Blahnik took the wedding pictures. After Tina gave birth to daughter China, the Chows moved to Beverly Hills to open a second restaurant, and after son Maximillian was born, they moved to New York to open a third. >

Tina Chow wearing her own vintage Fortuny gown to an AIDS trust charity gala at Christies, London, in 1987. Her punk haircut and ultramodern Lucite and black bangles demonstrate her knack for styling an old piece so it looks brand-new.

< The New York Mr. Chow was more like an exclusive dinner party than a restaurant, where guests such as Jean-Michel Basquiat, Andy Warhol, and Stephen Sprouse held court, drinking champagne and pushing rice around their plates. (Not with chopsticks, however—Mr. Chow had forks, and Italian waiters.) Whenever chic foreigners were in town—maybe some members of Duran Duran or Signor Valentino—they headed to Mr. Chow for a night out with the in-crowd. Tina hovered wispily over the endless party like a sophisticated hummingbird, wearing either a super-casual pair of Kenzo pants, a T-shirt, and a cardigan, or an ultra-elegant vintage couture getup. She was by turns a pioneer of minimalist chic, with her slicked-back boy-short hair, and a fashion person's fantasy paper doll, in full Kabuki makeup.

Although Tina inspired her contemporaries in fashion, she curated for herself, over her short life, a signature yet comprehensive wardrobe of vintage couture. Remember, this was well before it was chic to wear things a second time around. To find her cherished pieces, she had to canvass thrift shops and flea markets, not simply poke through the racks at some luxe boutique. But ever since her husband had given her a Fortuny gown early in their courtship, Tina had been in love with vintage, and she made scouting and restoring it her passion.

As the years went on, the Chows grew apart. Michael withdrew into a depression, and Tina became the public face of the family restaurants. When it was clear the marriage wasn't going to survive, Tina indulged in two love affairs: one with the actor Richard Gere, with whom she shared an interest in Tibetan Buddhism, and one with an aristocratic playboy who, she soon learned, was HIV positive. By then, he had passed the virus on to her. Long an AIDS activist, Tina had lost many members of her inner circle to the disease, and she knew what to expect now that she had been diagnosed.

Never hiding her diagnosis, even at a time when AIDS victims were stigmatized, Tina wanted her misfortune to serve as a warning to those nonchalant about having unprotected sex. Foregoing Western medicine for macrobiotics and meditation, she moved back to Los Angeles and streamlined her lifestyle. Her final project was helping to mount an exhibition of her vintage collection to be shown at the Fashion Institute of Technology. Harold Koda, now the head of the Costume Institute at the Metropolitan Museum of Art in New York, co-curated the exhibition. Tina wanted the show to be about the clothes—not about her—so students would be given the opportunity to understand the craftsmanship and concepts behind the collection she adored. "She wanted the students to see the differences between Dior and Balenciaga," Koda told *New York* magazine in 1992. Because of her, they did. >

She was by turns a pioneer of minimalist chic and a fashion person's fantasy paper doll, in full kabuki makeup.

< Where Tina Chow ruled uptown's downtown scene, Debbie Harry would have looked like a space alien were she to venture above Fourteenth Street. The lead singer for new-wave pioneer group Blondie starting in 1974, Harry had been a Playboy bunny and a waitress at Max's Kansas City before big success allowed her to commit to the musical life full-time. It was the delicious contrast between her cut-glass cheekbones and bleached-blond hair, her elegant figure and crazy rock style, that made Harry's look and persona so compelling.

By the time Blondie had their first number-one hit with "Heart of Glass" in 1979, Harry had been the muse of designer Stephen Sprouse for four years. Harry and Sprouse had met while living in the same building on the Bowery. "My friend had a loft above a liquor store," he told the *New York Times* in 1984. "We all lived on different floors, but we shared a kitchen that had a hot plate. Debbie Harry lived there and she would feed my cats. She was afraid they'd die in the winter and get stuck between the floors. Then I started cutting up these dance tights for her and helping her dress." His vision put her on countless magazine covers, and secured her eternal status as the queen of new wave.

Harry had a curvy but still somehow fleshless body that allowed her to look cool, not vulgar, in Sprouse's revealing clothes. Whether she was wearing a tight black minidress whose cutouts showed off triangles of her slim midriff, or a white sheath bound in red masking tape stripes, she managed to communicate a complex message that was part pinup, part femme fatale. Harry has had millions of imitators in the years since she rose to icon status, but no one has been able to make neon, bleach, and eyeliner look as *natural* as she did.

Harry had a curvy but still somehow fleshless body that allowed her to look cool, not vulgar.

Debbie Harry, lead singer of Blondie, photographed in 1980. "I know how stubborn and how committed I was to presenting an image—because I come from a time when women were less outspoken, and they had to follow along and not be as individual," Harry told her admirer Lady Gaga in an interview for *Harper's Bazaar* in 2011.

While society's grand dames glided up and down Madison Avenue in column dresses, their daughters ducked into the southbound subway in bubble skirts.

Uptown/Downtown

Whether uptown or downtown, in the 1980s, designers began to showcase the body more aggressively than ever before. This shift from obscuring the female form to emphasizing it—even augmenting it—was especially apparent in contrast to the diaphanous seventies looks that had been popular just a few years earlier.

While society's grand dames glided up and down Madison Avenue in meticulously draped column dresses, their daughters ducked into the southbound subway in bespoke bodices and bubble skirts. What did the looks of these two generations have in common? A new emphasis on the hard-earned hardbody, resulting from the fitness craze exemplified by fitness muses Jamie Lee Curtis and Olivia Newton-John.

For uptown girls, fashion functioned as cultural capital. Clothing needed to look expensive and to show off the shoulder, arm, and back muscles perfected during their personal training sessions. The designers who best understood the uptown aesthetic came from within it.

Oscar de la Renta was a designer living the life of his well-heeled clients. His marriage to socialite Annette Reed in 1989 put him at the epicenter of Park Avenue society. De la Renta knew how to make a serious ball gown, seeing no contradiction between the adjectives "sexy" and "appropriate." Because they were built on the couture foundations of the great Cristóbal Balenciaga, with whom

de la Renta interned, his dresses were the ultimate in quality and luxury—the closest thing New York had to couture. With intricate gathers, ruching, and bouquets upon bouquets of floral prints, de la Renta's dresses were always romantic and inspired by the Latin American world from whence he came. His creations were best modeled by women who had the luxury to remain relatively still, while others flitted about taking care of the details of daily life. >

Right The body that launched a thousand Jazzercise routines: Olivia Newton-John as photographed by über-paparazzo Ron Galella in 1980. The Australian sensation was taping a television special called *Hollywood Nights* at ABC in Century City.

Overleaf Shown here in 1983, it's obvious why actress Jamie Lee Curtis was cast as the lead in a movie called *Perfect* as the archetypal aerobics instructor.

DANGER

CURVES AHEAD

< Carolyne Roehm, a designer who at one point was de la Renta's fit model, was married to power broker Henry Kravis—one of the most influential players in New York finance. Because Roehm was both the designer and the client, she knew what her friends wanted out of an evening gown. Her architectural column dresses were body-conscious but not too revealing, with the goal of allowing the tennis set to show off their figures without being mistaken for pinups.

Bill Blass was the Svengali of the ladies who lunch, presiding over La Grenouille and other hoity-toity New York boîtes like a star quarterback in a high school cafeteria. Very much a self-made man who came from modest Midwestern beginnings, Blass admitted to affecting a slight British accent in order to elevate people's perception of his background. Although he catered exclusively to the fanciest of ladies, where Blass innovated was in sportswear, combining menswear elements such as pinstripes and plaids with more feminine silhouettes. His dressy aesthetic tended toward the matronly, with lots of cashmere, silk, and serious collars.

More for mistresses than for matrons were the drapey creations of Emanuel Ungaro. No one could whip a mumsy floral print into a tantalizing frock better than this French flower-power wizard. He perfected the art of the dart to sneakily play up the female form with his coquettish confections. With intricate bustiers, ruching, and a strong emphasis on bust, hips, and bottom, Ungaro proudly highlighted the ladybits. When asked about the difference between the French and the American idea of sexiness, comedian and cultural critic Fran Lebowitz said, "The French tend to use their tongues more, don't they?" One can only guess what she meant by this, but it seems oddly relevant to the delicate designs of Ungaro: He somehow managed to create a more seductive vibe with ruffles than many Americans did with spandex. Ungaro's designs dressed a woman so that it was still possible to *undress* her.

Vicky Tiel's dresses were also more likely to end up on the mistress than the wife. Strapless, ruched, and short, her party-ready creations epitomized the eighties ethos that sex sells, and they brought more than a little bit of naughty to the "nice" girls. >

Ungaro's designs dressed a woman so that it was still possible to *undress* her.

Above Azzedine Alaïa designed this dramatic, low-backed purple gown in 1984, the year that he won the awards for best designer and best collection at the Oscars de la Mode in Paris. Grace Jones carried him onstage for his big moment.

Right Valentino party guests Francesca Von Thyssen and Jerry Hall celebrate at members-only Annabel's nightclub, London, in 1987.

Downtown natives chose sleek, spare, form-fitting silhouettes that erred not on the side of too much fabric, but of too little.

In the 1980s, many of the best parties took place in washrooms. Legend has it that one could achieve a contact high simply by sitting upon a commode at the Ritz or the Limelight, two discotheques in downtown New York City.

< While champagne was spilling all over priceless dresses at parties on the Upper East Side, downtown Manhattan was abuzz with the spirit of punk. From Alphabet City to Tribeca, the East Village to SoHo, the soundtrack of downtown life was either loud and frantic like the Ramones, or hypnotic and seductive like Blondie. Visual artists such as Jean-Michel Basquiat, Keith Haring, and Julian Schnabel were treated like rock stars, and their gallery openings were as much about looking at the people on display as they were about appreciating the paintings. Downtown was where big money mixed with big ideas, and where cool rich girls like Cornelia Guest ventured away from home to pave their own way in fashion.

Where their mothers chose to show off the strength and femininity in their arms, shoulders, and cleavage, the daughters of prosperity, by donning long, often one-shouldered gowns, were all about showing a little leg. After all, they were doing some serious dancing!

Fabrice Simon, purveyor of party dresses, was one of the first designers to bring the uptown girls downtown, signaling the migration of fashion in the same direction. Candy confections concocted from beads, sparkles, and hand-painted crepe de chine, Fabrice's dresses had but one aspiration: to party. No surprise, then, that Fabrice himself was a frequent high-profile escort to society girls in need of a date—and quite frequently, the girl was Cornelia Guest, who, as a bubbly, leggy blond, served as his de facto muse. "My mother doesn't like me to look too sophisticated. And I agree," an eighteen-year-old Guest told *People* magazine. "I don't need a big ruby necklace to make me feel outgoing. There's plenty of time for jewels when I'm in my twenties."

While uptown girls who ventured downtown favored whimsical, shrunken versions of the over-the-top styles their mothers wore, downtown natives were embracing a different sensibility entirely. They chose sleek, spare, extremely form-fitting silhouettes that erred not on the side of too much fabric, but of too little.

For serious fashion insiders more likely to be found at Studio 54 than the Jazzercise studio, Azzedine Alaïa designed what we have come to think of as the platonic form of the little black dress: form-fitting jersey with figure-enhancing details such as faggotry stitching, ingeniously placed seams, and clever cutouts. Alaïa's love for the female form may have stemmed, in part, from the fact that he was once employed as a costumer for the Paris burlesque institution Crazy Horse, but his biggest fans went from being career dancers to world-famous supermodels when he opened his eponymous house in the late 1970s. >

< Another designer who began his career as a costumer for Parisian exotic dancers was Patrick Kelly, an American enfant terrible who took Paris by storm when he decided to become a part of the couture syndicate. Kelly fell in love with fashion as a boy, when his grandmother, who worked as a domestic, brought him glossy magazines abandoned by the women she worked for. He must have expected to have to fight for his place in Paris, but the Chambre Syndicale, the federation of French couture designers, welcomed him with open arms, charmed by his whimsical creations and ebullient spirit. Kelly's designs had an impressively broad appeal, pleasing both nineteen-year-old supermodels and aging screen icons (see Bette Davis in her Eiffel Tower dress). Whether he was working magic with buttons, ribbons, or zanily colored zebra stripes, Kelly's presence as a young, streetwise African-American man in the highfalutin couture scene was game changing.

Designer Patrick Kelly in 1987, with his models in Paris. Kelly was respected by the old guard for his vision and craftsmanship, and by the new kids for his whip-smart subversion of cultural norms.

The eighties offered the most vivid visual environment since the sixties— graphic, Technicolor, high-affect, loud. While some designers applied art to fashion and others treated fashion as art, the vibrant dialogue between fashion and visual media lasted the decade.

Whether for the sake of pure aesthetics or as a declaration of fashion's social value, some designers took art off the wall and moved it onto the body.

Yves Saint Laurent had game-changing ideas for every decade over the course of his career, but in the eighties, it was his use of art and graphics that was innovative. He applied iconic images from Picasso to Gauguin onto his dresses, reinforcing his conception of fashion as fine art and inserting his own work into the Western canon.

The downtown New York scene was obsessed with the work of art star Keith Haring, emblazoning items head to toe with his iconic doodles so that SoHo girls blended right into the graffitied billboards in their neighborhood.

The perception of fashion as art originated with European nobles and royals hundreds of years before, and lived on in France's vibrant haute couture tradition, especially through young virtuoso Christian Lacroix. Like Americans Bob Mackie and Mary McFadden, Lacroix viewed fashion as the pursuit of creating wearable art, not just dressing people. And in the 1980s, society was more than willing to elevate the high level of craftsmanship and vision required by one-of-a-kind clothing to the status of high art.

Lacroix brought younger customers, and a breath of fresh air, to couture. Many credit him with resurrecting a grand tradition that had begun to wane in the 1970s as sportswear experienced its renaissance. The bespoke confections created by Lacroix radiated drama, grandiosity, and the aura of meticulous hand-workmanship, and clients such as Blaine Trump shelled out tens of thousands of dollars for a custom piece that could be worn only once, then likely archived in the collection of a major museum. For someone like Trump, commissioning a Lacroix was akin to acquiring an important painting: an investment in the primacy and legacy of his vision. >

Art as Fashion/
Fashion as Art

Right The most elegant—and the richest—women in the 1980s wore Yves Saint Laurent. While his sensibility in the seventies was considered avant-garde, by the eighties, YSL had become the label of the establishment. A cape encompassing as much yardage as this one only suits a lady of leisure.

Overleaf Christian Lacroix in 1988 with his models, who are wearing ensembles from his first haute couture collection.

McFadden did more than just outfit her peers.
Her deliberateness and intellectuality pushed
fashion forward.

< Bob Mackie, he of the jewel-encrusted, skimpy ensembles, is perhaps the last person one would initially associate with Lacroix. But on closer examination it's clear that the two men worked in similar ways, and shared common beliefs about the goals of their chosen profession. Responsible for creating what was perhaps the most memorable red carpet look of all time—Cher's midriff-bearing showgirl outfit, in which she accepted the 1988 Academy Award for Best Actress—Mackie had a background in costume design, and it showed. He was the first and last person to create suspense on the red carpet—what was he going to do next? From the sheer volume of flesh he was willing to unveil, to the intricately placed rhinestones and embroidery that not only embellished his pieces but also provided some much-needed camouflage, Mackie's creations left fans breathless with anticipation every time one of his muses was set to make a public appearance.

Given her background, Mary McFadden would seem a likely patron of Mr. Mackie, but instead of buying his dresses, she created her own. The daughter of a cotton broker and a socialite/concert pianist, Mary McFadden culled design ideas from the numerous arenas that composed her incredibly eclectic life. She studied sociology and ancient ethnic cultures in college, and her pieces reveal these influences. Her Fortuny pleating techniques were inspired by the fashions

of ancient Greece and Egypt, and, of course, by Señor Fortuny y Madrazo himself (see page 38). The architectural precision and superb structure of her designs—as well as her references to ancient cultures—lent them a gravitas and timelessness rarely present in clothing from this time. (When you see a Lacroix or a Mackie, it's clear that it originated in the eighties.) Although frequently lumped together with the scores of other designer/socialites, McFadden did more than just outfit her peers. Her deliberateness and intellectuality pushed fashion forward.

Above Just another lazy afternoon at the family castle back in 1982: models Nancy Donahue and Joan Severance wear ensembles designed by Mary McFadden and Oscar de la Renta, respectively.

Overleaf Thierry Mugler's Cadillac bustier of 1989: Nobody needed to remind the gentlemen to start their engines when a lady was walking around—or rather, lying around—dressed like this.

One wasn't sure who the joke was on when clients spent thousands of dollars on outfits emblazoned with "waist of money" or "I'm full of shirt."

Action/Reaction

The eighties were the decade when popular culture became political. Live Aid, Farm Aid, ACT UP, We Are the World . . . Everywhere you looked, artists and activists partnered for a common cause. Undoubtedly the spirit of these collaborations grew out of sixties hippie culture, but now artists taking a stand took a more militant, rather than stoned, approach to making their points.

Two groups of fashion designers took two diametrically opposed approaches to dealing with issues of the time, which ranged from famine to AIDS, poverty to nuclear power. A British group proactively and provocatively made clothing that—often literally—made a statement, while a Japanese group made subtle visual choices that quietly commented on—and condemned—attitudes of the dominant culture.

British designer Katharine Hamnett's modern, graphic message tees captured the zeitgeist of a new brand of glamorous activism, one that wished to distinguish itself from the messy political fashion statements of the hippie seventies. And her convention-flouting made news: The image of Hamnett meeting Margaret Thatcher in a political tunic was printed all over the world, and remains one of the iconic images of the 1980s.

Also using words in fashion was Franco Moschino, but where Hamnett took aim at politics and culture, Moschino was interested in challenging and lampooning the very arena in which he worked. Where Hamnett was cool and provocative, Moschino was a loudmouthed comedian. One wasn't sure who the joke was on when clients spent thousands of dollars on outfits emblazoned with "waist of money" or "I'm full of shirt."

Epitomizing the innovation and risk taking that characterized London's music scene in the late seventies and early eighties, Vivienne Westwood's work was always bold and insouciant. By sampling motifs from such diverse worlds as the plaid-bedecked Scottish Highlands and the punk mecca of the King's Road in London, Westwood created a mishmash of tradition and rule breaking that captivated fashionistas well beyond Great Britain. She made the punk rock aesthetic commercial, primarily by making her crazy clothing inarguably sexy. Westwood brought the angst of punk music onto the runway—and the punk agenda into the real world.

But some serious fashion people were wary of walking around in corsets with safety pins protruding from their earlobes. As Fran Lebowitz said at the time, "I think punk fashion is fine if you are nineteen years old. For anyone older, it exhibits the basest sense of longing." Those who agreed with her still had powerful, statement-making options when choosing their wardrobes. >

Right Two strong, minimalistic swimsuits designed by Katharine Hamnett. Part mod, part tribal, all fashion.

Far right Katharine Hamnett's message tees on the runway. Hamnett was also responsible for George Michael's iconic "Choose Life" shirt, made famous in the Wham! video "Wake Me Up Before You Go-Go."

< Although Rei Kawakubo's work has never fit my personal aesthetic—I like glamour, while she favors apocalypse—I have great respect for her ability to articulate the feeling of malaise swelling under all the celebration throughout the mid-eighties. Her austere, deconstructed, sometimes sad pieces seemed to be a reaction to the Cold War. Her clothes weren't sexy, but cerebral— and as such, they are highly collectible today as not only wearable art but also sociological artifacts. And one could argue that it was the gestalt of Kawakubo's work—somber and monotone, with unexpected details and focus being pulled away from the contours of the body—that would lay the foundation for the cool, monochromatic look that dominated the 1990s.

The Western variation on Kawakubo's post-apocalyptic theme came in the form of Claude Montana's inverted triangle silhouettes. Montana's women were drama personified—tall warriors in white leather. His designs managed to be simultaneously demure and devilish, with a strange sophistication that made them totally unique.

On a hanger, this holey Comme des Garçons sweater would look like a giveaway. But on the body, it transforms into the definition of post-apocalyptic glam. According to the brand's founder, Rei Kawakubo, "Fashion is something you attach to yourself, put on, and through that interaction the meaning of it is born. Without the wearing of it, it has no meaning, unlike a piece of art."

Rei Kawakubo's austere, deconstructed pieces weren't sexy, but cerebral.

Left A look from Stephen Sprouse's bridge line, S, in 1987. His take on American sportswear was game changing. Who would have guessed that a patriotic palette could look so rebellious?

Right It wasn't necessarily the individual pieces Sprouse designed, but the way he put them together, that made his point of view seem so new. A blazer and shift dress combo sounds like an outfit that would suit a schoolmarm, but in Sprouse's hands, such a getup was better suited to a delinquent (of course, the white fishnets didn't hurt).

DESIGNER OF THE DECADE

Stephen Sprouse

A talented American who brought a true street sensibility to high fashion, Stephen Sprouse scribbled graffiti all over his design—and all over the establishment. After a brief stint at the prestigious Rhode Island School of Design and an apprenticeship at Halston during its heyday, Sprouse began his solo career dressing Debbie Harry and the rest of Blondie in body-conscious outfits he created from dance tights.

Like his mentor, Andy Warhol, Sprouse knew how to parlay his iconic sensibility and provocative message into commercial buzz. Soon he was creating a wildly expensive, hand-painted collection from Italian textiles, and selling to the finest stores in New York: Henri Bendel and Bergdorf Goodman. With a black-and-Day-Glo palette diametrically opposed to the beiges and taupes that ruled the early-eighties runways, Sprouse's high-affect clothes—and attitude—made waves among the most stylish members of the downtown scene. His model roster read like the VIP list at CBGB or Max's Kansas City: Patti Smith, Steven Meisel, Iggy Pop, Tama Janowitz. In addition to Debbie Harry, Sprouse found a muse, collaborator, and spokesperson in the form of the statuesque Teri Toye, an openly transgender woman who starred in his campaigns and runway shows. In Sprouse-world, androgyny was sexy, no matter what one's personal proclivities.

Fluorescent pink minidresses, canary yellow stockings with leopard-print crotches, skintight jeans emblazoned with stars and stripes in red, white, and blue: Sprouse's looks brought new meaning to the words "graphic design." He created many of his iconic prints on a color Xerox machine he kept in his apartment (in Sprouse's time and milieu, possessing such a machine would have been akin to having a 3-D printer today), and collaborated with artists Keith Haring, Andy Warhol, and Jean-Michel Basquiat to produce witty, larger-than-life looks that blurred the boundaries between art and fashion.

What Sprouse had in vision and craft, he lacked in business sense, so despite strong sales and critical acclaim, his label suffered multiple bankruptcies and relocations. Still, his influence was profound: Sprouse's sharp, mod shapes and Day-Glo nonchalance still turn heads today.

The 1990s

At the beginning of the century's last decade, the fashion world began experimenting with a technique hip-hop artists had employed for years: the art of sampling. In hip-hop, sampling meant combining a hook from an old song with a beat from a new one—creating something entirely original in this unique combination, whose sum was greater than its parts. In fashion, sampling translated to taking pieces out of their expected context and transplanting them into a foreign one. Women began tossing Chanel jackets on with their jeans and T-shirts; shuffling around in beachy flip-flops under their bias-cut Galliano gowns. Dressing became a game of High/Low.

In 1996, Sharon Stone wore a Gap turtleneck with a Valentino ball skirt to the Academy Awards. That evening, she rewrote the definition of getting dressed up. Until then, women had gone either "dressy" or "casual"—but never before had they combined the two to form a wholly idiosyncratic red-carpet look.

Revolutionary as it was, Stone's Oscar ensemble arose out of a fashion emergency, not a master plan. The year 1996 marked the beginning of the era when designers started lending actresses dresses to wear at awards shows, in a gesture of mutual marketing support. Stone had been looking forward to wearing a gown by Vera Wang, but by the day of the awards, it still hadn't come. So she was forced to raid her own closet, in which she found a fabulous trumpet skirt by the great Valentino, but no top to go with it. She threw on her favorite Gap turtleneck in the world's most basic shade of gray, and became one of the world's best-dressed women.

Women began tossing Chanel jackets on with their jeans and T-shirts.

Previous A Thierry Mugler multicolor dress in an undulating pattern, from his spring/summer collection in 1990. The serene pattern shows a tame side to the Austrian designer, who became famous for his woman-as-warrior take on high fashion.

Right In the nineties, women began sampling designer logos like rappers sampled hooks. Crown Princess of the mix was multi-platinum recording artist Lil' Kim, captured here by David LaChapelle in 1999.

More than a wardrobe stylist,
Patricia Field is like an art director
for the body. For this shoot in 1991,
she has brought a contemporary
twist to a melange of mod staples.

Patricia/Carolyn

The art of combining fashion opposites
was pioneered by mixmaster Patricia
Field. Today, the Technicolor-tressed
Field is widely known as the costume
designer for *Sex and the City*. But
before Sarah Jessica Parker became a
fashion icon, Field was a punk pioneer
with a touristy drag-queen shop in
downtown New York.

It was Field's ability to get the mass
audience excited about fashion that made
her such a pivotal figure in the nineties, the
era in which luxury brands' business strategy
was to go from aspirational to accessible.
"*Sex and the City* has succeeded in creating
an exclusive club of a billion women around
the world who all speak the same language.
It liberates their fantasies and imagination,"
Field told the *New York Times* in 2010.
(Think about it: Do you know a woman who
isn't fluent in Blahnik?) Even though many
of the pieces Field chose for her fashionista
characters were out of reach for the average
woman, she made names such as Jimmy
Choo and Christian Louboutin part of the
conversation in households hundreds of
miles away from stores that carried them.

Field was unafraid to treat the world
of style like a Vegas all-you-can-eat
smorgasbord, grabbing a scoop of haute
couture here and a shake of hoochie-mama
there, to create a postmodern mélange
of references and price points. In *Sex and
the City*'s opening credit sequence, Sarah

Jessica Parker's Carrie is wearing a blush
pink tutu while loping through the grimy
streets of New York. An MTA bus—one
plastered with an advertisement featuring
her own image, of course—douses Carrie's
perfectly fluffy femininity in dirty gutter
water. We cringe for the poor skirt. We're
not sure where she got it, but judging from
the looks of the oh-so-fabulous Carrie,
it must be couture, right?

Wrong. It just looks that way. Fashion is all
about context. According to Field's sometime
collaborator on the show, Rebecca Weinberg,
that iconic tutu skirt cost just five dollars
and was cloned by the show's costume
department so no one would have to worry
about it getting damaged in multiple takes.
Field makes a witty visual commentary on
our perception of the preciousness of high
fashion when that skirt is soiled. Do we feel
less—or more—sympathy for clotheshorse
Carrie in a cheap ruined skirt or an
expensive one? The 1990s taught us to
challenge all our preconceptions of style,
demonstrating that what at first may seem
superficial can be deceptively powerful. >

Carolyn Bessette-Kennedy and John F. Kennedy Jr. in 1999. Carolyn's low-key style was surprisingly under-documented: Memorializing the "American Princess" in *Vanity Fair*, Evgenia Peretz wrote, "Perhaps the reason that Carolyn never quite achieved Jackie's fashion-icon status was that she never really wanted to. For Carolyn . . . life was simply too much fun for that."

< On the opposite end of the New York fashion universe from Field was Carolyn Bessette-Kennedy. Where Field's aesthetic was one of mania, humor, and sharp social satire, Bessette-Kennedy was the epitome of straightforward elegance. Where Field, with her Manic Panic hair and wardrobe of runway samples, cultivated an image that was firmly rooted in the now, Bessette-Kennedy's angelic face, goddess body, and timeless style gave her an eternal appeal.

Bessette-Kennedy gave up a career in fashion to marry John F. Kennedy Jr. on September 26, 1996. For years, as a single beauty in New York, she had been steeped in the cool, fluid austerity of Calvin Klein, in whose publicity department she had worked. When she became a free agent, though—wedded to no particular designer—she made an effort to incorporate a wide array of talent in her closet. Sometimes she aimed to demonstrate that designers often regarded as esoteric and difficult—Yohji Yamamoto, for example—were actually more subtle and sensible than people had been led to believe. Other times she brought talented young designers to the fore: The collaboration that forever changed the wedding gown industry was her commission to a young Narciso Rodriguez.

Mr. and Mrs. John F. Kennedy Jr.'s wedding portrait is a paean to American glamour. The bride is ebullient in profile, her flaxen hair smoothed into a casual bun at the nape of her neck, her lithe, classical figure skimmed by the purest of bias-cut gowns. "The inspiration for the dress was Carolyn—simple as that," Rodriguez told me recently. "She had great personal style: cool, sophisticated, and modern. I had the most beautiful muse I could ask for, and she gave me license to be creative. I really admired Carolyn. She not only had a broad knowledge of fashion, but she also had a natural sense of knowing what suited her, and being able to edit. The ability to look at clothes this way is innate. For a designer, it's a very exciting moment to meet a woman like that. A woman who knows."

Bessette-Kennedy's approach to style was a function of both her intellect and her instinct. She had the face of a long-gone screen icon, the kind of vaguely ethnic, sumptuous beauty possessed by legends such as Dietrich and Garbo. Even though it's been more than a decade since her tragic death, photographs of Bessette-Kennedy seem to improve with age, just like the crystal-clear, streamlined lines of Rodriguez.

Where Field's aesthetic was one of mania, humor, and sharp social satire, Bessette-Kennedy was the epitome of straightforward elegance.

A twenty-three-year-old Cindy Crawford has the run of the place in a bustier-top dress by Jean Paul Gaultier. By the early nineties, Crawford had begun hosting *House of Style*, the groundbreaking MTV show that brought fashion to a mainstream audience.

Supermodels/Waifs

Even though the austere glamour of Carolyn Bessette-Kennedy was at odds with the super-consumerist gloss of the supermodels—a.k.a. Linda, Naomi, Christy, Claudia, and Cindy—she shared with them a ripe, healthy beauty that most women in the late eighties and early nineties strove to emulate. Bitten lips, sultry eyes, strong brows—these gals were the picture of healthy estrogen levels. They walked the runways and graced the print campaigns of high-octane glitz-makers like Versace or Dolce and Gabbana, and *Vogue* made sure that everyone in the world knew they wouldn't bother getting out of bed for less than ten thousand dollars.

George Michael's "Freedom! '90" video, a slick black-and-white spectacle directed by the now-famous film director David Fincher, showed the supermodels in various states of sublime beauty, lip-synching the song. Of course no viewer could mistake the soulful man-voice as belonging to one of these girls, but seeing them "sing" Michael's music seemed somehow natural. The video pointed out the fact that we wanted these women to sell us everything, from pouf skirts to pop songs. We had been trained to expect their faces everywhere, and we weren't complaining. Supermodels were the personification of the American dream: the Statue of Liberty come to life and stripped down to her push-up bra. >

<u>Now fashionistas imagined themselves zoned out in a Seattle garage, smoking cigarettes and listening to Nirvana.</u>

Kate Moss's gamine beauty was refreshing in its classic appeal. Her slight frame and girlish face meant that, in this photograph from 1993, Moss could look fully dressed wearing nothing but a knit body stocking.

< The supermodels were the women everyone wanted. Technically, the waifs were the ones nobody wanted. Until the 1990s. The literary definition of a waif is a child separated from his or her home by tragic circumstances—a figure whose loneliness is heartbreaking but whose survival instinct is sneakily strong. The waif models of the 1990s were aptly named. Who would think that a country conditioned to revere the Alaïa-clad glamazon could be so transfixed by a beige speck of a girl in beat-up jeans?

Kate Moss appeared in a Calvin Klein jeans campaign with Mark Wahlberg—a.k.a. "Marky Mark"—back in 1992, at the same moment that the public's fantasy drug of choice went from cash to heroin. The ultimate fashion environment was no longer a pimped-out suite at some over-the-top Philippe Starck hotel filled with white couches and mirrored coffee tables. Now fashionistas imagined themselves zoned out under Buffalo-plaid throws in a Seattle garage, smoking cigarettes and listening to Nirvana.

Marc Jacobs's grunge collection for Perry Ellis, which he presented in 1992, put flannel shirts, Converse, and Birkenstocks on the runway. The collection was so negatively received by critics and fashion buyers that Perry Ellis shut Jacobs's line down in its wake. Only a sucker would pay thousands to purchase a designer look they could compose for free from their grandpa's closet. That was Jacobs's point. Unfazed by the critical reaction, he later told the *New York Times* that the morning after the grunge show was one out of only two post-collection awakenings when he didn't find himself depressed.

The grunge collection immortalized a cultural moment. The economy was winding down as the United States began to lose its eighties bloat. Top Forty stations played Nirvana, not DeBarge. And Calvin Klein anointed a short, skinny, stringy-haired British teenager as the new Brooke Shields.

"There was . . . this new kind of beauty that was starting to be recognized," Jacobs told *Index Magazine* in 2000. "Girls like Kate Moss. There was this idea of the shoe-gazer, this person who couldn't look up, who's sort of insecure. And I've always felt like that, that I never fit in. But that's sort of empowering too." Empowering, indeed—almost twenty years later, Jacobs is still running at the front of the fashion pack, having made it over in his own image.

With so many gay men living in fear of AIDS in the early 1990s, women were cast as the new sexual adventurers (see *Sex*, by Madonna). Gianni Versace designed clothes that were meant to do one thing if they did nothing else: seduce. Dolce and Gabbana, too, reveled in the traditional Italian conception of womanhood.

When you saw a girl in a Versace dress, you knew what she wanted: some jewels and a yacht, preferably both hand-delivered. The desires of a Miu Miu or Marni coveter were not so clear. Was she sporting that shapeless, expensive sack in order to create desire or squelch it? Was she aware that the piece she'd fought so hard to score didn't do a thing for her figure?

It's fascinating that both Miu Miu and Marni—which quickly became known for their stubborn insistence on cloaking feminine assets in boxy shapes and nubby fabrics—were helmed by Italian women. One can only assume that they were engaging in a dialogue about feminism in a country that had dramatically glorified and reduced women for centuries. Miuccia Prada, for Miu Miu, and Consuelo Castiglioni, for Marni, created collections that functioned as tests of a woman's beauty. (If a girl gets that covered up, in such drab fabrics, and still manages to get laid—she has passed.)

The designer who knew how to market and sell sex better than anyone else in the 1990s was an American who reinvented an Italian brand: Tom Ford. Taking the reins of the Gucci brand in 1994, not even thirty-five years old, he turned a struggling leather goods company into a wildly successful force of global commercialism. Ford had—and still has—an uncanny ability to distill a label to its DNA, and to rebuild it on its original foundation to create a brand with renewed integrity. Ford knew that in order to rebuild an iconic brand, one needed to relaunch an iconic item. Moments after they were released, his bamboo-handled handbags—a chic mainstay of the first generation of American Gucci customers in the 1960s—were on the shoulders of *Vogue* and *Harper's Bazaar* accessories editors. They soon migrated to the wardrobes of debutantes and fashionistas all over the country. Ford had gotten these women to trust him. Once he unveiled the sexy cutout jersey dresses, wildly embellished denim, and velvet tuxedos that made the new Gucci instantly iconic, the world forgot that the old Gucci had never been known for its runway collection. Ford made it seem as though these wholly authentic-looking pieces had been lurking in a gold-plated vault at company headquarters, waiting to be rediscovered. >

Hypersexy/Dowdy

Supermodels Linda Evangelista, Christy Turlington, and Helena Christensen wearing Versace in around 1992, photographed by Herb Ritts. A year earlier, Evangelista had told *Vogue*'s Jonathan Van Meter, "We don't wake up for less than ten thousand dollars a day."

Previous In this photograph, titled
My House, aesthetic rabble-rouser
David LaChapelle captured the
vibrance and beauty of a Christian
Lacroix couture gown worn by Alek
Wek for *Paris Vogue* in 1997.

Left There's nothing virginal about
this white dress, photographed by
Mario Testino in 1996. Tom Ford's
sensuous edge revitalized the Gucci
brand in the 1990s by mixing sex
with Gucci's thoroughbred heritage.

< In addition to knowing what the new
Gucci needed to look like, Ford knew how
to market it. The double-*G*s branded as its
own prime cattle a select group of women
such as Madonna and Gwyneth Paltrow,
intelligent beauties who were known for
their sophistication and willingness to take
risks. The day after Madonna wore Gucci
velvet trousers to the MTV awards in 1995,
every woman between the ages of eighteen
and forty-five was on her way to buy a pair
of velvet pimp pants, cut to elongate her
leg and to draw attention to her flanks with
their dangerously low rise. Ford didn't care
whether she bought the originals or a
moderately priced knockoff. His goal was
to create epic desire for a brand that could
then make billions through the sale of
"hard goods," a.k.a. accessories, and "juice,"
known to most as perfume. His reinvention
strategy turned Gucci from bankrupt to
wildly profitable in record time, and made
him the architect of the fashion business's
new foundation.

In 1999, hungry to replicate the success of
Ford's turnaround, Gucci bought Yves Saint
Laurent's eponymous label and charged Ford
with working his magic again. In 2000 he
rose to the challenge, reincarnating Saint
Laurent's house as "YSL" and putting
Mombasa bags on the shoulders of young
fashionistas and their mothers, just as he
had done with bamboo handles years earlier.
On their sleek bodies he draped transparent
layers of leopard-print silk, bare gypsy
dresses, luxe leather jackets. Loyal fans
of Monsieur Saint Laurent took sides against
Ford, saying his hypersexual, trend-driven
vision cheapened a house that had always
been known for its integrity—and whose
founder was still alive to witness it. But
the bags sold regardless.

Deconstruction/Embellishment

Left With its bare and spare construction, and a halter knot which conjures up both a necktie and a noose, this look by Ann Demeulemeester (worn by British model Stella Tennant) recalls the punky androgyny of a seventies Patti Smith.

Above A look from the runway show for Ann Demeulemeester's 1997 spring/summer collection. "I start with the idea of a movement," she told the *Guardian* that year, "and this season I wanted to have the nonchalance of something falling down."

While the mass market wanted to wear the heart of its favorite brand on its sleeve, a core group of tastemakers was swinging the other way. Downtown girls such as esoteric filmmaker Sofia Coppola and indie rock goddess Kim Gordon built avant-garde wardrobes based on subtle innovation, subversion of shape and palette, and a dash of punk. Designers who espoused this vision moved past minimalism and into the realm of deconstruction.

Ann Demeulemeester was one of the Antwerp Six, a group of Belgian designers who found fame in London in the late 1980s. With her slim pants, chunky heels, and layers of asymmetry, Demeulemeester perfected the vaguely post-apocalyptic, snobby Goth aesthetic that still rules the closets of fashionable, cutting-edge intellectuals today.

Daryl Kerrigan, a hard-lined Irish beauty who was the unofficial queen of New York's East Village throughout the nineties, dressed her girls in postmodern biker drag. Her chic leather outerwear and pants were found in the same wardrobes as Demeulemeester's darkly ethereal creations. Roughly a decade later and on the opposite coast, Rick Owens would propose a similarly dark and powerful vision for Hollywood's avant-garde starlets in pursuit of the ultimate anti-starlet wardrobe.

One collection that no starlet, no matter how fashion savvy, chose to wear on the red carpet was Comme des Garçons' 1997 "Lumps and Bumps." Designer Rei Kawakubo presented a series of geometric dresses strategically stuffed in certain areas to exaggerate female body parts. Although the pieces could be read as a commentary on the role of the female body in fashion, some chose to see them as a conceptual exercise. As Cathy Horyn wrote in the *New York Times*, "Some designers, like Alber Elbaz of Lanvin and Azzedine Alaïa, solve problems of dressmaking—putting darts in a skirt to give it softer volume. Kawakubo, working more in the spirit of an artist than any designer today, attacks the problems of consciousness."

The groundbreaking fashions of the mid- to late-1990s were postmodern in their self-referentiality, provoking fascinating conversations between eras. But the most intellectually compelling garments aren't always the most flattering to a woman's beauty, especially when worn on the red carpet. Björk proved her bravery when she chose to wear that infamous Marjan Pejoski swan dress to the 2001 Oscars, but she didn't exactly look glamorous. She might have chosen a vintage Surrealist Schiaparelli, which, while still conveying wit, would have shown off her exquisite face and figure, rather than the stuffed swan's.

Narciso Rodriguez began his solo career with a bang when he designed his best friend Carolyn Bessette's wedding dress (see page 225), but he was no overnight sensation, having trained under Donna Karan at Anne Klein, and Calvin Klein, then serving as design director of Cerrutti and TSE. "The Dress" debuted when Carolyn and John F. Kennedy Jr. were married in 1997. By the following year, Rodriguez had launched his eponymous label, as well as taken over design duties at Loewe.

Although made famous by "fancy" evening looks, Rodriguez had a classic American sportswear pedigree. He incited a quiet revolution with his fresh take on daytime separates, replacing stiff button-down shirts with sleek knits, and trading in restrictive slacks for floor-dusting bias-cut skirts. Despite being unfettered by ornamentation, and often made from menswear fabrics, Rodriguez's designs exuded a classic femininity because their shapes always derived from the natural curves of a woman's body.

Born into a tight-knit, matriarchal Cuban-American family, as a child Rodriguez dreamed of being an architect or fine artist. "I learned from my mother and my aunts that you could use your hands to make beautiful things out of nothing," he once said.

Rodriguez enrolled at the Parsons School of Design while he was still in high school, then quickly scored an apprenticeship at Anne Klein, under the tutelage of Louis Dell'Olio and Donna Karan. From Karan, he learned about draping and sketching, and developed a pure love of fabric. Rodriguez then moved to the house of Calvin Klein, which he has described as "a finishing school of sorts." It was there that he met Carolyn Bessette, Calvin Klein's in-house publicist. When she decided to get married, it was a given that Rodriguez would design her dress. Neither of them thought of it as that big a deal. "But it was a great moment in our personal lives that generated a tremendous amount of attention," Rodriguez says.

Since his most famous design's debut, Rodriguez's label has epitomized the expression of intelligent, minimalistic, yet highly feminine fashion. Longtime fans such as Claire Danes and Jennifer Connelly have repeatedly chosen to wear his designs on the red carpet, probably because they bring attention to the beauty of the woman, not the beauty of the dress. "The House of Narciso stands for . . . the great dress that a woman depends on . . . her favorite go-to dress. I like to touch people's lives beyond something that's going to appear in a magazine, and then you never see it again . . . I love it when I see a woman wearing 'vintage' Narciso because it makes them feel as good today as it did when they first got it."

DESIGNER OF THE DECADE

Narciso Rodriguez

A 1997 ensemble by Narciso Rodriguez, shot by Carter Smith for *Harper's Bazaar*. When Narciso Rodriguez got done baring a woman's midriff, it hardly looked bare at all. Rodriguez proved that the fact that a look was minimalist didn't mean it couldn't also be sexy. He created feminine clothing that smart women wanted to wear.

The Decades
Decade

Previous Detail of a Christian
Lacroix Haute Couture origami
gown in purple satin from the
2000s. "We all look for lost time,"
Lacroix once said.

Left Decades muse Marisa Tomei
wearing Christian Dior New York,
a diffusion line that offered couture
looks to a wider audience in the
1950s. At the time this dress was
made, Yves Saint Laurent was the
head designer at Dior. He was also
the only assistant Christian Dior
ever had.

Wearing vintage showed that a woman had respect for history and tradition.

The 2000s in fashion really began on September 11, 2001, when the planes hit the towers on the last day of New York Fashion Week. Editors milling around the tents in Bryant Park, waiting for the shows to start, witnessed a monumental puff of powdery smoke and ash rise above lower Manhattan. They removed their stilettos and walked uptown among the droves, their barefoot, well-manicured feet bleeding into a cloud of dusty work boots and flimsy flip-flops.

The attacks of September 11, and the politics, division, and wars that followed, brought a gravity to the fashion industry that it hadn't seen since the Second World War. Critics found themselves unable to focus on the European shows, devoting their column inches to cultural commentary rather than the dissection of hemlines. Style-obsessed New Yorkers had no use for the frivolous. Politics polarized relations between global fashion capitals in Europe and the United States. Designers presented collections that were more successful as opinion pieces than wardrobe staples. The early 2000s were a bad time to try to sell new clothes.

But life went on, and women still needed to get dressed. Unlike commissioning new haute couture, which might be perceived as a distasteful reminder of conspicuous consumption, wearing vintage showed that a woman had respect for history and tradition.

Vintage couture provided a vessel through which one could pass into a happier time:

When this dress was made, New York hadn't yet been torn apart, and a pack of Juicy Fruit cost a quarter. Back when she was my age, my grandmother might have worn a dress exactly like this one.

Maybe because of the showiness some associated with exorbitant high fashion, denim began to infiltrate every echelon of modern life. Where in previous cultural crises, Americans had turned themselves out in somber, polished formal daywear as a sign of seriousness, post-millennial custom made dressing down a lifestyle choice. The change was immediately evident in the numbers: Jeans sales were $13.4 billion in 2001, up by nearly 5 percent from the year before. >

This photograph of model Ruby Aldridge, taken by her half-brother Miles Aldridge for *T* magazine in 2011, illustrates high fashion's thrift-store-ification in the new millennium. While her dress is by Dior and her coat is by Gucci—complemented by accessories from Hermès and Patek Philippe—the whole getup could believably have come from a fantasy Salvation Army shop in the sky.

They just don't make fashion like they used to. Thank goodness they don't, or I'd be out of business.

< In a global climate where denim and despair ruled, fashion designers frequently chose to play it safe by revisiting old ideas: their own, those inspired by personal nostalgia, or those taken direct from the company vault. If the 1990s were the era of the sample, the 2000s were the era of the remix.

Fashion moves in cycles, cycles that—regardless of political or social ennui—refer back to past trends. Much of the fashion of the eighties harkened back to the forties. In the nineties, kids dressed like their parents had, back in the seventies.

In the 2000s, this cycle of reference sped up. Starting a new century seemed to collapse all the eras of the old one into a collage of nostalgia. People yearned to relive moments from the era that had passed. Many of the most popular movies were remakes and sequels. Broadway marquees advertised a neon sea of revivals. Sales of comfort-food cookbooks soared. And fashion houses plumbed their archives to rerelease the iconic pieces that had defined their brands in the twentieth century.

As designers demonstrated over and over again via self-referential homage, they just don't make fashion like they used to. Thank goodness they don't, or I'd be out of business.

A dress belonging to a different time gives a woman permission to leave today's problems behind. Like a time-travel suit, vintage couture affords her entrance into dimensions beyond her own realm. She can change her pedigree, or insert herself into a mythology she admires. Even if not born into the tradition to which she aspires, she can become a part of history with just a pull of a zipper. Wearing vintage can be the ultimate tool in the act of self-(re)creation. "Vintage fashion can be an escape," Nicole Kidman told me recently. "You can both lose and express yourself in it."

Many of the twenty-first century's fashion trailblazers are often described by words like "tastemaker" and "arbiter," rather than "designer." Polly Mellen, the creative director of *Allure*, labeled Tom Ford a "great editor" when he debuted his first collection for Gucci back in the nineties. Mickey Drexler, the genius behind Ann Taylor's, the Gap's, and J. Crew's most successful incarnations, rose to the front of the specialty-store pack because of his knack for mixing the nostalgic with the new. Sarah Lerfel, who owns the Paris boutique Colette, fills her shop with a judiciously chosen array of goods that have no common characteristic other than that they've captured her imagination—and as a result, the imaginations of the world's migratory fashion pack.

Even when overwhelmed by sartorial static, a style visionary can filter out what looks new, and what looks tired. Which pieces, recontextualized, grow in significance and reflect some insight into the current fashion dialogue, and which pieces, resurrected, feel dated and retro. >

< I feel fortunate that I built my own business on this ethos back in 1997. Until quite recently, with the launch of Decades Denim, Decades for Modern Vintage shoes and Decades for Miriam Haskell jewelry, I had never designed things under my own moniker. Even though I've done design consulting for a number of heirloom brands, I have always considered myself to be more of a curator than a creator. Opening a salon filled with one-of-a-kind objects that compelled me was a labor of love as much as it was an adventure in commerce.

But at the same time, I am a purveyor, not a collector. Unlike a curator of fine art, I covet objects whose meaning and relevance depends entirely on someone wearing them. Clothes are meant to be worn. When these pieces from the past are worn with great reverence, they come alive, in a different way from how they would look behind a glass vitrine. Yes, they are museum-quality, but the Decades client wears them with reverence and respect, thus becoming her very own archivist.

Spectacular old gowns possess the same aura emitted by black-and-white movies, iconic screen stars, and *really* good jewelry. They effervesce, they compel, they mystify.

People often say, "If these dresses could talk, just imagine the stories they'd tell!" To me, these dresses *can* talk. You just have to know how to listen.

Spectacular old gowns possess the same aura emitted by black-and-white movies, iconic screen stars, and *really* good jewelry.

Left This look from Gucci's 2010 collection, designed by Frida Giannini, not only incorporates the complex DNA of Gucci's brand—fine equestrian craftsmanship with Fordian S&M overtones (see page 230)—but also manages to blaze new territory with its powerfully feminine point of view.

Above In the ultimate act of celebrity decadence, Sarah Jessica Parker collapses onto the floor of Silvercup Studios wearing Versace Couture, during filming for the final season of *Sex and the City* in 2004. She was styled for the show by the inimitable Patricia Field.

Index

Claire McCardell's influence is evident in this design by Tomas Meier for Bottega Veneta, photographed in 2012. Like Louis Vuitton, Bottega Veneta is an established accessory house that has successfully transitioned into ready-to-wear with the help of a young visionary.

NOTE: Page numbers in **bold** refer to photographs.

About the Author

Since **Cameron Silver** opened the doors of Decades in 1997, the dress code in Los Angeles has irrevocably changed, due—in large part—to Silver exhorting his frequently-photographed, trendsetting clientele to "dress up!"

Creating looks from deep within the closets of Decades, he styles celebrities for major red-carpet appearances, including the Golden Globes and the Academy Awards. His impact on runway trends is widely recognized, and he has acted both as public emissary for fashion houses and as secret weapon, consulting on everything from re-imagining a brand's identity to maneuvering its global launch.

Named one of *Time* magazine's "25 Most Influential Names and Faces in Fashion" in 2002, Silver is a favorite commentator on national television networks. He has also written about luxury (from travel to his front row perch at haute couture presentations) for publications including *Harper's Bazaar* and *C* magazine. He is currently filming his new television series, as well as developing further projects for Decades and beyond.

For more information, visit **www.decadesinc.com**

Dita Von Teese is the personification of what I always imagined Decades could be: thoroughly rooted in the present, with a sophisticated awareness of—and a new take on—the past.

Picture Credits

p.2 Cecil Beaton/© Condé Nast Archive/Corbis; p.4 PA Archive/ Press Association Images; p.6 © Douglas Friedman; pp. 8, 14–15 © Amanda Friedman; pp.16–7 akg-images, London; p.18 Digital Image 2012 © The Metropolitan Museum of Art/Art Resource New York/Scala, Florence; p.19 photograph by Hulton Archive/Getty Images; p.21 private collection/by courtesy of Julian Hartnoll/ The Bridgeman Art Library; p.22 photograph by SSPL/Getty Images; p.24 photograph by Jacques Boyer/Roger Viollet/Getty Images; p.26 photograph by Fratelli Alinari/Alinari Archives, Florence/Alinari via Getty Images; p.27 photograph by Hulton Archive/Getty Images; p.29 © L'Illustration; p.30 photograph by Bassano/Getty Images; p.31 © White Images/Scala, Florence; pp.32–3 © Amanda Friedman; p.35 akg-images, London; p.36 photograph by Imagno/Getty Images; p.37 photograph by Roger-Viollet/Rex Features; p.38 Frances Benjamin Johnson/© Corbis; p.39 © ullstein bild/TopFoto; p.40 photograph by FPG/Getty Images; p.41 photograph by Moffett © Corbis; p.42 photograph by Ira L. Hill/FPG/Getty Images; p.45 photograph by Keystone-France/Gamma-Keystone via Getty Images; p.46 dpa Picture-Alliance/dpa; p.47 Friedrich/Interfoto; pp.48–9 © Victoria and Albert Museum, London; pp.50–1 © Amanda Friedman; p.52 © John Springer Collection/Corbis; p.53 photograph by Library Of Congress/Getty Images; pp.54–5 photographs by Edward Steichen/© Condé Nast Archive/Corbis; p.57 photograph by Hulton Archive/Getty Images; p.58 by kind permission of The Fitzgerald Museum; p.59 photograph by Popperfoto/Getty Images; p.61 Kobal Collection; p.62 akg-images, London; p.63 © ADAGP, Paris and DACS, London 2012; p.64 Topham Picturepoint/Press Association Images; p.65 The Granger Collection, NYC/TopFoto; pp.66–7 © Amanda Friedman; p.68 photograph by Topical Press Agency/ Getty Images; p.69 photograph by Horst P. Horst/© Condé Nast Archive/Corbis; pp.70–71 © ullstein bild/TopFoto; p.73 photograph by Eugene Robert Richee/John Kobal Foundation/Getty Images; p.75 photograph by Nickolas Muray © Nickolas Muray Photo Archives; p.77 akg-images, London; p.78 photograph by Cecil Beaton/© Condé Nast Archive/Corbis; p.79 photograph by Baron De Meyer/Mary Evans/National Magazines; p.80 dpa Picture-Alliance; pp.81–3 akg-images, London; p.85 photograph by Lusha Nelson/© Condé Nast Archive/Corbis; pp.86–7 © Amanda Friedman; p.88 © ClassicStock/TopFoto; p.89 © Sunset Boulevard/Corbis; p.90 Universal/ The Kobal Collection/Estabrook, Ed; p.91 © Bettmann/Corbis; p.92 akg-images, London; p.94 The Kobal Collection; p.95 © Bettmann/ Corbis; p.96 © John Springer Collection/Corbis; p.97 photograph by Silver Screen Collection/Getty Images; p.98 Roger-Viollet/Rex Features; p.100 photograph by Gjon Mili/© Condé Nast Archive/ Corbis; p.101 © Genevieve Naylor/Corbis; p.102 photograph by Serge Balkin/© Condé Nast Archive/Corbis; p.103 photograph by John Rawlings/© Condé Nast Archive/Corbis; p.104 © Jerry Cooke/Corbis; p.105 © Genevieve Naylor/Corbis; p.106 photograph by Horst P. Horst/© Condé Nast Archive/Corbis; pp.108–9 © Amanda Friedman; p.111 akg-images, London; p.112 photograph by Loomis Dean/ Time & Life Pictures/Getty Images; p.114 photograph by Gjon Mili/ Time Life Pictures/Getty Images; p.115 photograph by Horst P. Horst/© Condé Nast Archive/Corbis; p.116 © Sunset Boulevard/ Corbis; p.118 akg-images, London; p.119 photograph by Archive Photos/Getty Images; p.121 photograph by Henry Clarke/© Condé Nast Archive/Corbis; p.122 photograph by Frances McLaughlin-Gill/ © Condé Nast Archive/Corbis; p.123 © Genevieve Naylor/Corbis; p.124 photograph by Francesco Scavullo/© Condé Nast Archive/ Corbis; p.125 photograph by Frances McLaughlin-Gill/© Condé Nast Archive/Corbis; p.126 photograph by Henry Clarke/Condé Nast Archive/Corbis; pp.128–9 © Amanda Friedman; p.131 ullstein bild/ AISA; p.132 Dennis James/Rex Features; p.135 photograph by Larry Ellis/Express/Getty Images; p.136 photograph by William Claxton/ Courtesy Demont Photo Management; p.137 photograph by Sal Traina/© Condé Nast Archive Corbis; p.138 photograph by Sante Forlano/© Condé Nast Archive/Corbis; pp.140–141 RA/Lebrecht Music & Arts; pp.142–143 akg-images, London; pp.144–145 photograph by Bert Stern/© Condé Nast Archive/Corbis; p.146 © 2005 TopFoto; p.147 photograph by David McCabe/© Condé Nast Archive/Corbis; p.148 photograph by Keystone Features/Getty Images; p.149 photograph by Lionel Kazan/© Condé Nast Archive/Corbis; p.151 MGM/The Kobal Collection; p.152 © TopFoto; p.153 © Steve Schapiro/Corbis; p.154 photograph by Patrick Lichfield/© Condé Nast Archive/Corbis; p.156 © Norman Parkinson Ltd/courtesy of Norman Parkinson Archive; p.159 photograph by Franco Rubartelli/© Condé Nast Archive/Corbis; pp.160–1 © Amanda Friedman; p.163 © Norman Parkinson Ltd/courtesy of Norman Parkinson Archive; pp.164–165 © Duffy; p.167 photograph by Eva Sereny, Camera Press London; p.168 photograph by Walter Iooss Jr./Contour by Getty Images; p.169 photograph by Keystone/Hulton Archive/Getty Images; p.170 © Steve Schapiro/Corbis; p.171 photograph by Francesco Scavullo/ © Condé Nast Archive/Corbis; pp.172–173 © Estate of Guy Bourdin. Reproduced by permission of Art + Commerce; p.174 Dirck Halstead/ Time & Life Pictures/Getty Images; pp.176–177 © Duffy; p.179 © Estate of Guy Bourdin. Reproduced by permission of Art + Commerce; pp.180–1 © Norman Parkinson Ltd/courtesy of Norman Parkinson Archive; pp.182–3 © Amanda Friedman; p.185 photograph by Denis Piel/© Condé Nast Archive/Corbis; pp.186–187 © Julio Donoso/Sygma/Corbis; p.189 © The Andy Warhol Foundation for the Visual Arts/Artists Rights Society (ARS), New York/DACS, London 2012; p.190 Richard Young/Rex Features; p.193 © William Coupon/Corbis; p.195 photograph by Ron Galella/WireImage/Getty Images; pp.196–197 © Douglas Kirkland/Corbis; p.199, above, © Estate of Guy Bourdin. Reproduced by permission of Art + Commerce; p.199, below, Richard Young/Rex Features; p.200 © Estate of Guy Bourdin. Reproduced by permission of Art + Commerce; pp.202–203 © Julio Donoso/Sygma/Corbis; p.205 © Norman Parkinson Ltd/courtesy of Norman Parkinson Archive; pp.206–207 © Julio Donoso/Sygma/ Corbis; pp.208–209 photograph by Denis Piel/© Condé Nast Archive/Corbis; pp.210–211 © Julio Donoso/Sygma/Corbis; p.213 by kind permission of Katharine Hamnett; p.213 photograph by Peter Jordan/Time Life Pictures/Getty Images; p.214 © Peter Lindbergh; pp.216–7 photographs by Thomas Iannaccone/© Condé Nast Archive/Corbis; pp.218–9 © Amanda Friedman; p.221 photograph by David LaChapelle/Contour by Getty Images; p.223 © Alen MacWeeney/Gallery Stock; p.224 photograph by Ron Galella/ WireImage/Getty Images; p.226 photograph by Wayne Maser/ © Condé Nast Archive/Corbis; p.228 photograph by Terry O'Neill/ Getty Images; p.231 © Herb Ritts/Trunk Archive/courtesy of Versace; pp.232–233 © David LaChapelle/Art + Commerce; p.234 courtesy of Gucci/© Mario Testino; p.236 Kim Knott/Vogue © The Condé Nast Publications Ltd; p.237 photograph by Niall McInerney, Bloomsbury Fashion Photography Archive, Bloomsbury Publishing Plc; p.239 © Carter Smith/Art + Commerce; pp.240–1 © Amanda Friedman; p.242 © Ted Soqui/Corbis; p.245 © Miles Aldridge/Trunk Archive; p.246 © Jason Kibbler/Trunk Archive; p.247 © Molly Rogers; p.248 © Kai Z. Feng/Trunk Archive; p.253 photograph by John Sciulli/WireImage.

Acknowledgments

In 2007, in the car on the way to the Nancy Reagan retrospective in Simi Valley, California, bestselling author Jean Stein said to me, "You should write a book." Suddenly we were on the phone with her—and eventually my—literary agent, Bill Clegg. Two weeks later, I had a book deal. Thank you, Jean, for your encouragement, and Bill, for helping me to envision what "my history" of fashion might look like in print.

Into my life Bill brought Rebecca DiLiberto, who has been absolutely instrumental in choosing every word and picture in this book. She's joked that *Decades* took practically a decade to write, and I've cherished the post–farmers' market Sunday sessions when we would meet to discuss each decade of fashion. Rebecca brilliantly made sense of my pontifications. Rebecca, you are the greatest partner in literary crime and a true friend.

At Bloomsbury, I have had the unwavering support of my editor Richard Atkinson and his brilliant associate Xa Shaw Stewart, with whom I've shared some magical moments of Skype'd ménage-à-trois (always while I was eating, for some reason).

Production wizard Marina Asenjo has ensured that *Decades* is as luxurious as possible. Lisa Silverman and Rachel Mannheimer at Bloombury USA have also been instrumental in keeping me on deadline and then some! The publicity duo of Ellen Williams in the UK and Sara Mercurio in the U.S. have been tireless in promoting *Decades*, along with the bubbly gang of Scott Cooke, Phyllis Roback London, and Mara Estes at GCK. It takes a village, doesn't it? I have no idea what photo editor Heather Vickers looks like, but she knew exactly what I wanted *Decades* to look like . . . no small feat. Pete Dawson at Grade Design took my abstract directions on the design of *Decades* and managed to translate them into what I hope is a tome for the ages. Christos Garkinos and our team at the Decades boutique have been very patient with my oft-distracted "I am on deadline" barrages. In particular, Jarred "Lil' Jer Jer" Cairns, who is like a brother, and Eri Hoxha, my Albanian princess, were essential to the cover shoot. The clothes came to life through the sharp eye of generous photographer Amanda Friedman, her assistant Todd Weaver, and my dear friend Patrik Milani. Hugh Devlin has been the ultimate attorney and advisor, and I promise to follow whatever he suggests until the end of time . . . he knows best.

Finally, to Jeff Snyder, who has had the distinct privilege and punishment of being part of this process from start to finish: I couldn't have done this without you. Thank you for sharing and carrying; smiling and shining; and being my better half since 1998.

Fashion must be new.
Rudi Gernreich, 1968

If it's in fashion, it's already old.
Cameron Silver, 2012

For my parents, Jack and Margot Silver, who inspire me,
and whom I love "more than words can wield the matter."

First published in 2012

Text copyright © 2012 by Cameron Silver

The moral right of the author has been asserted

All rights reserved. No part of this book may be used or reproduced in any manner
whatsoever without written permission from the publisher, except in the case
of brief quotations embodied in critical articles or reviews. For information, please
address the publisher

Bloomsbury Publishing Plc, 50 Bedford Square, London WC1B 3DP
Bloomsbury USA, 175 Fifth Avenue, New York NY 10010

Bloomsbury Publishing, London, New Delhi, New York, Sydney

A CIP catalogue record for this book is available from the British Library

Cataloging-in-Publication Data is available from the Library of Congress

UK ISBN 978 1 4088 0636 4
US ISBN 978 1 5969 1663 0

10 9 8 7 6 5 4 3 2 1

Design: Peter Dawson, www.gradedesign.com
Cover photograph: Amanda Friedman, www.amandafriedman.com

Printed in Italy by Mondadori

All papers used by Bloomsbury Publishing are natural, recyclable products made from
wood grown in well-managed forests. The manufacturing processes conform to the
environmental regulations of the country of origin

www.bloomsbury.com
www.bloomsburyusa.com